The Journey of One

The Journey of One

Jenifer Marie

The Journey of One

Copyright © 2017 by Jenifer Marie

All rights reserved. No part of this book may be reproduced in any form or by any electronic or mechanical means including information storage and retrieval systems, without permission in writing from the author. The only exception is by a reviewer, who may quote short excerpts in a review.

ISBN 978-1-935914-77-8

Cover art and design by Melanie Gendron

Interior design by River Sanctuary Graphic Arts

Printed in the United States of America

To order additional copies please visit:
www.riversanctuarypublishing.com

River Sanctuary Publishing
P.O Box 1561
Felton, CA 95018
www.riversanctuarypublishing.com
Dedicated to the awakening of the New Earth

*Dedicated to Nik, Brandon, and Cameron.
Thank you for teaching me the most important
life lesson of all: unconditional love.
I love you beyond the words.*

Contents

Preface 1

Introduction 5

Chapter 1. The Journey Into Love 11

Chapter 2. Loving the Goddess Within 23

Chapter 3. Thanking My Judas 41

Chapter 4. The Seeds of the Mind Grow in the
              Garden of Your Soul 47

Chapter 5. The Journey Out of Fear 53

Chapter 6. Living Life Consciously 73

Chapter 7. Heaven or Hell: A Present Reality 83

Chapter 8. "I AM Manifested" 91

Bibliography 103

"I AM"

I am more than what I see... more than what I think... and more than I can imagine.

I am full of beauty and grace awaiting exposure. I am life in all its fullness. I am all that I need inside... strong... determined... and ready!

I am LOVE. LOVE in its realest form because it dwells in the walls of my soul... Penetrates the chambers of my heart... and projects through my every action, word, or thought.

I am an amazing woman... demonstrating the characteristics all women contain, but fail to reveal.

I am enough... in everything I do... everything I say... And in all I dream.

~Jenifer Marie

Preface

Relax little one – you are already whole and perfect, and there is huge potential that is longing to create through you – just relax.

~Freedom IS, Brendan Bays

Our entire lives are spent searching, climbing, striving—only to wake up one day utterly exhausted. It is at this point we truly surrender and come to realize we are that which we have been searching for. We know ourselves as already whole and perfect when at last we unlearn the lies about ourselves we have been programmed with and remember the truth of who we really are. How different my life would have been if, as a little girl, someone would have whispered to me, "Relax little one —you are already everything you need to be and there is boundless potential within you that will bless the world."

Instead, most of us spend a good portion of our lives fighting to discover and finally reclaim that which we were born with but were conditioned to forget. This change is usually precipitated when life presents us with an *ah-ha* moment, a wake-up call — which only happens when you are ready or so past done (which is a more pleasant way of saying you've landed face down in the carpet) that you need to be shocked back into holiness.

I have always had a *knowing* there was something more, just not understanding what that feeling was pointing to. Then one day as I was walking through Target, the book , *Something More*, by Sarah Ban Breathnach jumped off the shelf and landed in my cart. I literally could not put *Something More* down and had to buy it. Up until that point, I did not even read for enjoyment, but my soul knew there *was* something more, and it was in a book that was now in my shopping cart.

And the words danced through my spirit: *"For now, it is time to begin the search. The pages are still blank, the Russian writer Vladimir Nabokov tells us, but there is a miraculous feeling of the words being there, written in invisible ink and clamoring to become visible."*

As I read these words I began to recognize the beauty our souls contain. My soul had always been whispering… live… write… love… but I was too busy trying to manage life to listen. I now know it is time to pay attention to life, discover the *why* behind it all, to fall in love with the beauty of words, to write with passion in order to help myself and others grow on this spiritual journey.

The Journey of One is a reflection of life lessons experienced by one person, culminating in the realization that when we recognize the "big picture," we can learn and move on instead of *scratch-repeat* like one of those old LP records that, stuck in a groove, keeps repeating over and over. In this book, I share my awareness of my lessons— which are a reflection of the ONE —presented through my own truth and understanding. We can overcome and move beyond those things that hold us captive in life by learning from each other's lessons. We learn that there are no mistakes, only life lessons that bruise and beckon us to continue to grow. By giving in to my own process, I discovered that when I reflect on this life and recognize that there is a bigger purpose for all of this, I can choose to heal and I can choose to love; which in turn gives others the choice to heal and to love. When you accept the *Journey of One* invitation, you acknowledge that you are ready to let go of the negative thought patterns about your life, about yourself, your poor choices up until this point, and you begin the process of peeling back the layers to learn the lessons necessary to move on.

My prayer is that this book will help you discover the beauty that is between your breaths and that you have a glorious purpose: to bless this world with your I AM presence, beginning right now. You are no longer bound by your past or held hostage by your future. You are in this beautiful moment now, that we share, in order to discover the *something more* within your story, which I already know is Amazing, Divine, and Exciting because God created you as such. So as we move forward together, grow together, cry together, write together, know that I am learning with you daily. It is the innocence of being human that renders us all equal and nudges us to remember and reclaim ourselves. We all must master and overcome this life, this mind, to Be who we are. It is not about the ones who we "thought" hurt us or attempted to destroy us, as a key part of our process is to move and grow beyond judgment.

Today, we are beginning to create our world from love not fear. As we move through the chapters of this book together, you will recognize that I have shifted from manifesting life experiences based in fear to creating my world by loving consciously. In the past, it was the not knowing that kept me in ignorance (a state of ignoring the truth), but even in the dark one can choose to light the eternal flame within the soul, rising to higher consciousness to see the world anew. Today, in our new state of awareness, we accept our lives as our classroom and we see those in our lives—

our teachers or our students—as all having a Divine purpose; and we give thanks for it all without judgment.

> *When the understanding surpasses the circumstance,*
> *then the healing can take place.*
>
> ~Jenifer Marie

When we can look at our lives with an aerial view, we begin to understand from that perspective. We can shift from victim mode and then the beautiful healing energy can be released.

According to the *Ascended Master Instruction*:

> *The power through self-conscious knowledge, gained through the life of experience, gives one infinitely greater capacity, greater understanding, greater power than the one who has never come into it at all.*
>
> ~Guy Ballard

When we look at our lives through this new lens of knowing, based on what we have experienced, our focus becomes one of healing so that we can begin to create our lives from the Source as intended. This is the truth of who you are and this is the moment to begin to approach life with a higher awareness of the Laws of Life and to create our world as it was intended to be—an expression of Love in a constant state of Love.

Introduction

As I write these words, it is something way beyond myself that moves my pen. The calling to write, to help, to change lives is a calling of the Divine. My journey has been full of many highs and lows, but has been my greatest classroom. It is said when the student is ready, the teacher will appear. In addition to that, when the student is ready, life will present opportunities for growth. It is very often that in despair or the depth of pain that we truly discover who we are and learn the life lessons essential for our souls. *The Journey of One* is a reflection of the life lessons learned during my journey thus far. This is my love letter to the world. No matter what you face currently in your life…there is a higher purpose in all things. If you are reading this book, then these words are meant to bless your soul. These are my spiritual arms wrapping around you, whispering to you, *"Hold on…you will see."* My prayer is that you will have the eyes to see and the ears to hear to find your answers…learn your life lessons…elevate your soul…and fulfill your higher purpose.

I have known for many years that this book would be written. It is a calling that continues to beckon, regardless of my current position in life. I was doing a Hemi-Sync meditation class one Saturday. I love Hemi-Sync meditation because it helps quiet this mind and has helped me to be silent. My focus during meditation was: *What is the purpose of my book?* I just put the question out there for my angels and guides to help me find a focus. As I counted down, all I could see was vast blackness and a whiteboard with the words clearly in BIG BLACK BOLD writing:

TO SEE GOD, TO RELEASE PAIN, AND TO BE HAPPY

When I came out of meditation, I just started laughing out loud. It is as if my angels understand how stubborn I can be and that I needed clear and explicit direction for the focus of my book.

As I was preparing my book proposal and conducting a market analysis, I discovered that the market revealed that most people are looking for one thing: Hope. Perhaps *hoping* to find it in the one book that would change your life and make sense of all of the unknown. "Hope" is defined as *a feeling of expectation and desire for a certain thing to happen*. But what exactly? We are all seeking to make sense of this life, this pain, and be forgiven by a God that is merciful so we can go to heaven. The Hope we are all seeking is to receive an understanding of the Truth, remember who we are, and find our joy in this life, now. We are all spiritual beings, having a physical human experience, learning life lessons, to remember we are spiritual beings. We are in this world but not of it, but seem to get stuck somehow along the way. So love, the purpose of this book is to help you and me see God in all things, release pain, and above all be happy in finding Hope beyond all Hope.

Recently, I went on a writing/meditation retreat to Mount Shasta, California, to finish this book. The cabin I stayed in was in the middle of the woods, in complete silence, with no outside distractions (Internet, cell phone, television, etc.). The most serene and beautiful quality about this cabin, other than the silence, was this amazing river that flowed beside it. I could hear the powerful flowing waters and it completely put my soul at peace. In the mornings, I would walk down to the river's edge where I would sit and meditate. I could feel the beautiful healing energy flowing from the healing waters. The realization that surfaced from my time there was this: our lives are like the river. There are many boulders, some big, some small, and the size determines how the flow of water (life) will happen. The boulders represent life lessons, which shape us on our life stream. If we do not learn our life lessons, then the big boulders can block the flow of water, much like a dam. Sitting by the river, my mind could observe how these boulders can block the flow of life's energy, making it more difficult for our life stream to flow. However, when we recognize and overcome the trials inherent in the lessons, we reclaim our power and our lives flow in their natural state toward Life's ultimate destination, which is back to the source or the ocean.

The Testimony
(Or the TEST)

How do we wake up one day and not recognize how we ended up here? The "whys" of the mind are continuous and will keep each of us asking the same questions over and over, if we allow this to happen. Our testimonies are our "tests" that teach us and wake us up to life's call. It is as if life has a way of hypnotizing us until something major happens and shakes us to *wake up*. Until then we sleep and we suffer. Until then we identify with every single detail of the story as if the justification of the details makes us more worthy of suffering. As if living my testimony wasn't enough, writing it became my teacher as well.

After I received the disappointing news from my attorney that I basically had to re-write this story in order to avoid potential litigation from the characters I had written about, I felt as if I had the breath knocked out of me. I experienced a profound sense of loss as I wondered, *Who am I without the details of the story? What gives me the right to write without proof? Haven't I suffered enough to be worthy of the words?* The truth is we all have suffered enough to be worthy of the words. I had to recognize and know that I am not the details of my story, but I AM the truth between the details. When you take all of the details away, all titles away, all beliefs away, there I AM. As I re-write this section, I write in the reflection of this question, *Who are we without the details of our story?* As I answer this question, I feel a shift to focusing on the universal truths between the details of the story. Instead of focusing on who hurt me, how they hurt me, why and what I learned, which is heavy and a low vibrating energy, I consciously shift to the Truth and Now, which is life; in order to offer the blessings of the words from this book without sending any negative intentions to anyone or anything.

In recognizing the steps of my journey, I can say it has not been easy, just as your journey probably hasn't been easy either. I have been married and divorced. I have been in relationships that have blessed my soul and I have been in relationships that have broken me down. I am a single mom and have known the struggle and the fear in the dark night. I have had a challenging childhood, emerging with a deep longing to understand. While all of these statements reflect a part of what I have been, none of them define who I truly am, unless I choose different. Everything that I have experienced in my journey has been completely necessary to bring me here, now, in this moment, writing these words.

In all brokenness, is the fullness of God. Life as I have known it has changed forever on many different occasions, during what I call the *ah-ha* moments. When necessary, life shifts to wake us up to a place where we can never go back. One of the best blessings is to begin to wake up to love. Love is the most important life lesson of all. Love is who we are. Love is the life energy that creates everything….from the magnificent sunrise, a bud into a beautiful rose, to the birth of every soul that embraces this journey. We all come from love, born into a world that has forgotten. So we forget. We become accustomed to the pain. We identify with that which is not who we are. The pain becomes our story. The pain becomes our excuse and our pattern. In our not knowing, we pass this pain or pattern on to our children, family members, friends, and those we encounter.

In an *ah-ha* moment, you can only look up or choose to give up. Something inside of me has always looked up with such starving curiosity that I had to seek the truth behind this life, God, Love, and understand my purpose. I had no idea that my search was beyond my own solitude and personal growth, but for each of you, which makes me eternally grateful and humble.

Chapter 1

The Journey Into Love

I want you to know beyond everything and with infallible confidence that you are more. You are not the pains of this world. Despite the fact that we all walk through despair at times, you are not the ache. I feel you cry into a thousand winds impenetrable across time. But you are not identified by the love you received or did not receive from your mother or father. You are not the abuse that still tries to silently destroy your soul. You are not the divorce or the brokenness, which scattered you into a million pieces. You are not the domestic violence and the anger that never seems to dissipate. You are not the longing and the emptiness of a career not chosen. You are not that pain which you identify with unconsciously on a minute-to-minute basis. Love, it is time to let go and release what no longer serves you. Love, it is time to awaken— awaken to your innate beauty and divine nature. Love, it is time to change the CD of the past, release its authority and control over your mind and BE free.

On this day, I say, Arise my love. Arise!

So, if we are not all the pain we have encountered, then who are we exactly? Why has it taken us so long to recognize that we are so much more, completely worthy of love in its most real form? Why have we struggled to even recognize what love means? Why has it taken eternities for us to wake up and realize that love is NOT outside of ourselves?

In the journey of One, love is our greatest lesson—the knowing beyond all knowing that you contain eternal love inside you, a love that is more beautiful and edifying than anything this world could offer. You are love manifested. Your journey into love is the opening of your spiritual eyes to see for the first time your angelic beauty within, without, and all around; a love that never ceases to exist. You are the luminous light of the world. The understanding that comes from love is to trust that everything you have walked through, each experience, has held a higher purpose, to teach you and take you higher on your spiritual path, regardless of the perceived pain. You are constantly learning and growing in this life. The journey of One into love is to comprehend that you and God are one, there is no separation, and there is nothing you can do to change that truth of life. You are the I AM, the arms and feet of God. Love is God in action and God is love in action, and you are the perfect picture of both.

As you read these words that I have written, words that may sound quite foreign or unfamiliar, you may be thinking that this applies to someone else, but not to you. But I ask you, "Why not?" We all come from the same source; we are all the same, souls on a learning course aiming to go deeper on this journey. If this is true, then why have we forgotten and how do we re-connect with our source— that which is love—so that we might understand the journey, and eventually overcome it?

I have spent my entire life identifying with love outside of myself. While I was growing up, love was how much attention I received from my mother, or did not receive from my father. It was always about how much another loved me. And even my definition of love, entirely based on my suffering and painful experiences and misperception, was about love outside of myself. Even after one divorce and one on the way, I was still looking outside of myself for the one special person that would love me unconditionally, my soul-mate. As a parent, I searched for love in my children and was determined (since all else had failed) theirs would absolutely be the "real" unconditional love.

I thought that unconditional love came from another person and I was not whole or right or perfectly normal until I found it. The search was endless and I would end up face down in the carpet, in the throes of hell, in a very familiar place, crying out to a God out there to save me and help me and show me the way. Not just once but many times, did I find myself in this situation, over and over again until one day I just stopped.

During my second divorce I was already seriously studying the spiritual teachings that are the basis for this book, so I made a commitment to myself that I would not date, wanting to concentrate solely on my project. When you are used to having others validate your existence, when you are looking for love outside of yourself, it isn't easy to stop seeing the opposite sex, especially when you need a boost to your self-esteem. This was my first step toward loving myself though, because I stopped distracting myself with the search and focused on self-healing and what God was trying to do in my life. What did I have to lose? I had already concluded that I had completely made a mess of my life, up until this point. Why not be alone for a little while?

For me, this was the dark night of the soul: undergoing a divorce, raising three boys alone, and being financially responsible for my household. But it was a first step, because unless we recognize the darkness, we will not have the awareness that change is needed or that light is required to improve or grow. Somehow we've heard a call that beckons to us, offering hope that we may mold our life into something better. So darkness is good love and the pain of life has a huge purpose. Thank God it does not last forever though, but if acknowledged, pain can change you and me for the good of all humanity.

My journey of One into love began the moment I made the choice to just BE and breathe— in the moment—to listen to that still small voice, that at times had been screaming, but I had ignored, until now. I could no longer disregard the knowing voice that was within me, the voice that said, *Jenifer there is so much more, be patient, trust the process and you will see.* I had no idea what it meant, but I knew that I had no other option but to be still and learn. In my search for hope I read many self-help and how-to books, all of which brought me—baby step by baby step—to this moment.

I meditated, not because I was brought up to meditate, but because I had to slow down my mind so I could hear; which meant I had to un-learn that meditation was wrong. My previous Pentecostal religion dismissed the concept of meditation. Now I was surprised to learn that the word "meditation" is defined as "prayer," so I meditated and I prayed. During this time, I became comfortable with being alone, which is a very difficult challenge for many. We are accustomed to stimulation— other people, a million distractions at once—and I was no different. I had to learn to be comfortable in my own skin, how to be by myself and like it, not love it yet, but like it. This was not easy though, especially when everything— including love—came from outside of myself, up until this moment.

I remember my children leaving for the first weekend after my separation and I did not even know what to do or who I was or why I didn't even recognize myself. I just lit some candles and turned on some music and tried to feel okay with this unfamiliar feeling. But this was my start, my beautiful beginning, my choice and commitment to myself, which sparked this amazing journey. So today, we start here, right where we are at, and choose to live and love differently.

In 1959, when he was seventy years old, Charlie Chaplin wrote the poem, "As I Began to Love Myself," about his life lessons. Here are some of my favorite lines:

> *As I began to love myself I found that anguish and emotional suffering are only warning signs that I was living against my own truth.*
>
> *Today, I know this is "AUTHENTICITY."*

In these lines, Chaplin's words reflect a higher awareness, a knowing, which identifies a reality within us all. All of our suffering and anguish is because we are living against truth. We do not have to wait until we are seventy years old though to wake up, rather we can choose to learn to live with a higher awareness, our true nature, today.

I absolutely resonated with every word of this poem, because in it Chaplin discovered his truth, his worth, his meaning, his beautiful love—which is a reflection of my own and yours. Identifying with the pain we have encountered, we truly do live against our own truth, our divine nature. But as we awaken to who we are, and why we are here, we align with our own undisputed origin. We align with our highest nature, which is God. The challenges we have faced are only here to take us further on the path, not to leave us broken.

As you awaken to your truth, the pains of the past will no longer bind you, no longer hold you back, and you can live free in the essence of who you are, which is LOVE. Know that you are exactly where you are supposed to be in this moment. Accept it. Recognize the truths of the situation you are in and learn why. Only then can you shift and go higher. In this realization is a powerful knowing. Wanting only leaves more wanting. However, desire is that which brings something new. Love with that desire for something more—and you will align and become your true self. I think of Anais Nin's quote, "And the day came when the risk it took to remain tight in the bud was more painful that the risk it took to blossom." This was me during my dark night, when staying the same and repeating the old patterns would only create more pain, but to choose to blossom or bloom into myself was far less of a struggle.

It is very easy to just keep existing in the comfortable place of pain that is so familiar. After all, you don't even have to think to be there and life goes on as you've always lived it…..albeit with longing. But there comes a point in our journey when the longing to live becomes stronger than the longing to exist in the pain. In that moment is more beauty than you can imagine. In that moment your soul is screaming for you to awaken and recognize who you are. Remember, it is in the brokenness that the beauty of life is formed. The small bud becomes the beautiful rose in all its fullness. This is who you are, love, life in all its fullness longing to be set free.

I grew up without my father. As a child, I remember the longing to be like everyone else. I remember feeling like something was wrong with me because my father didn't love me. As a child I bottled up the pain, ignored it, and tried not to hear the voice—whispers that always seemed to ask *why*.

At the age of nineteen, I got married and we took a cruise out of Cape Canaveral for our honeymoon. I knew my father worked at NASA, and once we came back to shore I was determined to see him. I had to find my answers and peace from the nagging questions. I asked my aunt to reach out to a friend who worked for NASA, to contact my dad.

The dinner was arranged. I remember the drive there and all the emotions stirring in my being. I remember sitting in front of this stranger, who looked so familiar. I watched his eyes, the way his lips moved when he spoke, the way he cut his steak and chewed. Numbness surrounded me as I witnessed. My longing for more was stronger than my longing to stay the same... aching... and unconsciously blaming myself, in all my innocence. I began to ask him the difficult questions. I wanted to understand this man on a deeper level, which is the only way I could release the past.

So I asked, "Why didn't you want to be a part of my life? Why don't you love me? Did you ever wish me a happy birthday silently, even though I never received a phone call or a card? Why did you have children if you never wanted to be a father?"

Then I listened intently to every word— his pain, spoken. He told me that he had grown up in an environment devoid of love. His father sent him to military school. When he wrote his father, the letter was returned with red ink correcting his mistakes in grammar. But what I heard was beyond his words. I heard his pain, his inability to love because of his past, the way he wasn't loved. I saw him, and recognized his agony as my own. This recognition didn't make any of the pain dissipate, but brought light into the darkness.

I was silent on the drive home from dinner. I was feeling deeply emotional, as my thoughts began to come together and my sense of knowing shifted. All I could think about was that my father did not know how to love me, because he was still a wounded little boy who was never taught how to be a dad. I realized then that it was *not* my fault and I had done nothing wrong.

Once we arrived at my grandmother's home, I went to my room, curled up in a fetal position, and cried. As I rocked back and forth the emotional weight from my childhood began to lift. All I could bellow over and over were the words, "I love my daddy… I love my daddy." As I cried, I released all of the lies that I had kept in the vault of my soul. These lies were daily reminders of why my dad was not in my life and why he did not love me. That little girl finally found her peace from an unexpected encounter with her father and in the flowing tears. I realized for the first time, people only love how they are taught to love, unless they CHOOSE differently. I choose to love differently. I choose love.

It takes tremendous courage to face your pain. It took tremendous courage for me to face a stranger who was my father, to seek the answers my heart had longed to know. I didn't realize it at the time, but this was my preamble into the journey of Love. Facing that which holds us back from loving or being more is the greatest gift we can give ourselves and others. The courage to choose love healed my heart and re-kindled my relationship with my father, while healing his heart from his past choices as well. The release healed us both and placed us both on a journey of Love, no longer held back by the pains of the past, simply facing the future anew. Because I chose to heal, I gave my father permission to choose to heal, which is something that took me by surprise. Our higher vibration gives others permission to raise their vibration too. I started to recognize how people choose to love, live, and grow, and it really does make a difference what one chooses.

There comes a divine moment in everyone's life when the power of love breaks through revealing the light of the soul. From that moment the shift manifests, igniting the flame that will light the world to see God.

~Jenifer Marie

What is LOVE? What is this powerful force that we all spend our entire lives trying to discover? All the while looking outside of ourselves, despite the fact that it's the very essence of every cell we embody? The Oxford dictionary defines *love* as: *deep affection, fondness, deep romantic or sexual attachment, great interest and pleasure in something; a beloved one.* Even the dictionary defines love outside of our selves! How can we blame anyone another moment for not recognizing who we are? I asked my niece who just turned three, "What is Love?" Her response: "Chicken fingers!" As I laughed out loud, I recognized that even at a young age, love is perceived as outside of ourselves. So now every time

I speak with her I tell her I love her more than chicken fingers, which makes her laugh from her eyeballs to her toes.

The Greek word for love is *agape*. "Agape" is defined as *selfless, sacrificial, unconditional love*, the kind of Love we receive from our source, or God. Agape is a motivation for actions that we are free to choose. Every Valentine's Day, I give my boys a Valentine's bag, red or pink, with a quote about love that I want them to know. A couple of years ago, the quote on their bags was: "You are LOVE mastering LIFE," which is the truth we all need to know. Beloved, you are the very essence of love. Love is in your innate being, the Divine within, and it's the foundation of this beautiful energy called Life. We are all on a journey of LOVE to master this life, which is our most important lesson. To understand who you are….the I AM within you, is to understand that you are LOVE. You are a manifestation of the DIVINE here to master life and to shine your light upon others.

> *Love is the bridge between you and everything.*
>
> ~Rumi

During my divorce, I would travel down to the Cape to spend weekends with my father when I didn't have the boys. These were quiet moments when I would attempt to regain strength and build my relationship with my father. My father is a very intelligent man. He has his doctorate in Physics/Quantum Physics, so conversations with him are always very interesting. During one of our talks we were deep in an exchange when I mentioned God. My father looked at me, the physicist looked at me, and said, "Everything that exists can be proven in a scientific equation, everything. So before you mention God again, prove to me that this God exists." I closed my eyes and said a prayer asking the Divine to give me the words to help me with my father. After several minutes of awkward silence, during which I could feel his stare sizing me up (even with my eyes closed), I opened my eyes and I locked eyes with Him.

I think he knew what I was going to say before the question even came out of my mouth. I asked him simply, "Do you love me?" I'm sure at this moment he was probably flashing back to our conversation at the restaurant. There was silence. A lot of silence. I could feel his mind working in overdrive. Finally, he looked at me intently and said, "Yes, I love you."

Then I said, "If everything that exists can be proven with a scientific equation, then prove to me that your love for me exists." My father looked at me, the physicist looked at me, and said, "I cannot prove my love for you in an equation, I just know."

I looked at my father and replied, "In that knowing is where God exists." From that moment on we have never raised the question or discussed if God exists. The understanding was made clear and the Divine gave me the exact words that my father needed to hear. I share this story because the essence of who we are is LOVE and LOVE is God, so there is no separation. We are Love. We are the I AM, knowing the essence of love, the essence of self, is Oneness with God. It's the beautiful moment when the I AM shines brighter than the flesh. The flesh is the thinking mind that wants to keep us separate from who we are. I believe this is what Rumi meant when he said *love is the bridge between you and everything* because you cannot separate you from me, or anything else in the universe.

Meditative Journaling

Welcome to Meditative Journaling, a process by which conscious considered thought is paired with the goal of seeing truth. Meditative journaling is writing from your soul, from that quiet place within, to discover and recognize what we need to know on a deeper level.

Instructions

Meditative Journaling should be done in a relaxed environment, with no distractions so the words and answers can flow from within.

To begin, ask yourself the following questions. Then let the answers flow onto the page:

1. *What is love?*

2. *How do I manifest love every day?*

3. *What has my greatest teacher taught me about love?*

Holding on to her last bit of hope, she gathered herself together, and prepared her heart for the bravest journey she would ever take…the journey back to herself.

~Unknown

More importantly…the journey back to loving herself.

Chapter 2

Loving the Goddess Within

With all that I am
and all that I may be
help me to release the
bonds so I may be set free.
Opening a heart ready to love
Discovering peace in a soul without rest
Hoping and praying for serenity
and nothing less.
With all that I am
and all that I may be
Realizing that I must love me.

~Jenifer Marie

One of the most important life lessons in the journey of One is to love the Goddess within. I have spent my whole life not doing a good job at this and perhaps you may have had difficulties with this too. Why is it so challenging for us to love ourselves, let alone the Goddess within? I wrote this poem in 2001, recognizing that I needed to love myself, but not manifesting this love in my life until 2015. Why did it take me fourteen years to learn to love the Goddess within me?

Your task is not to seek Love, but merely seek and find all the barriers within yourself that you have built against it.

~Rumi

I know that in my own life, loving myself had never been encouraged, taught, or modeled. *So, what exactly does it look like to love oneself completely; and what barriers have we built up against loving ourselves in order to stay complacent, comfortable, and small?* The barriers I have built have been driven by a need to maintain my past patterns of behavior, my struggle with perfectionism, and state of unknowing. Most of us love how we were taught to love, what was modeled to us by our parents, and how we interpreted love from the environment in which we grew up and based our awareness on. Until we rise up and awaken though, the patterns we live out are implemented unconsciously and rarely questioned. The moment we question though, we begin to take back our power and pull off the lid of our boxes to let in the light. We must ask ourselves, *Why do I think or do what I do, and for what reason?*

These are very relevant questions and asking them can help shift perspective in our lives so that we may start living from a place of love, so that we may begin loving ourselves fully and taking accountability for our own actions. Once one has the awareness, this knowledge of love and the goddess within, a divine calling beckons you to align to your own Divine nature; breaking the bonds of ignorance to begin the shift. Awareness of knowing is how I began to break through my negative patterns and go deeply into my God awareness.

~The journey of Love begins when one sees that beauty and love are within, has always been, and lights the world with wonder, healing, and imagination.~

~Jenifer Marie

The first step to loving the Goddess within is acceptance. We can gain acceptance by actually taking a moment to look within and discover the secret lies we have held for lifetimes. *What is it that I have needed to accept within myself, that I haven't up until this time?* In answering this question you may generate a list that is not surprising; in fact, the answers may sound all too familiar.

To begin with, I needed to accept that I am not perfect, because I have struggled with perfectionism for years. *Everything* in my life had to be perfect, including myself. This not only affected my own being, but affected my relationships as well. Merriam-Webster defines "perfectionism" as *a disposition to regard anything short of perfection as unacceptable; especially the setting of unrealistically and demanding goals; failure to achieve perfection as unacceptable and a sign of personal worthlessness.* Unbelievable! Leave it to Merriam-Webster to sum it all up so succinctly. Anything less than perfect for Jenifer was unacceptable; and to make it more poignant I would be reminded of my worthlessness daily, thanks to my mind's misperception. From believing that I had to be a perfect mom and a perfect wife, all while having a perfect body—no wonder I didn't know how to love myself! I was too consumed with trying to be perfect, but compared to what?

What had ever actually been perfect in my life? Or was this the unconscious reason I was striving to create this false illusion of perfection in my mind: to make up for all the imperfection I had experienced. Regardless, this is my starting point of acceptance—that I am not perfect, that I am enough, period.

What walls have I built to prevent my own acceptance? My "I am a single momma with no time for anyone walls." This was my safe place, behind those walls, where no one else could hurt me, with no awareness that I was hurting myself. With this restrictive belief I was limiting myself within time, to have this false illusion of protection, and to prevent the past from happening again. I did not even realize that my walls of prevention were the past happening again and again. But I was just like the Bill Murray character in the movie, "Groundhog Day," who finds himself in a time loop repeating the same day over and over. I did the same thing every day, with every relationship, including my relationship with myself, just to stay in that familiar place of pain and safety. Not realizing that my walls were even there, let alone that they were created by fear, or that with every new relationship there was a transference. Oh yes, what we don't heal and take care of now we definitely carry over to the next relationship or set of circumstances.

So my "protection mode" was basically, *"You're not allowed in mode."* I would let a person get just close enough to feel like I was healed and whole, but never truly reached a place of healing. It was like walking up to the edge of the ocean, but never sticking your feet in the water; just standing there dreaming of taking a swim, but turning away, never to experience it. Our minds have such a powerful ability to stay stuck in patterns, but thank God for our *ah-ha* moments. Those walls I created prevented me from loving myself for years because that which controls in fear cannot love. I felt safe within my walls, but they were actually my fears manifested in disguise. In order for me to truly love the Goddess within me, I had to release the fear, tear down the walls that provided a false sense of security, and see the Love that was within me, realizing that I was the one I had searched for all along.

I see with eyes that are not
afraid to see
The world as a view
Turning and hurting
Yearning to find the few
The ones who open their
souls to all that is
Discovering the truth
in life
in self
in mind.

Oh my eyes are shocked
to unravel the power
of self in the essence of time
Locked away in closets
tight to keep
Hiding the pain and hurt
we wish to not be
Only facing reality with every heart beat
Then understanding...in a moment
What is within me.

~Jenifer Marie

I think most of us spend our whole lives trying to accept ourselves as we are. Who told us that we were not perfectly made? "Accept" is defined as *acknowledge, receive with favor, take upon oneself,* or *to say yes to.* I love that last definition of accept: *to say yes to.* What is it within ourselves that we need to say yes to? Is it your body? Is it your past? Is it choices that you should or should not have made? Remember you are exactly where you're supposed to be… doing exactly what you're supposed to be doing and surrounded by those that are meant to be with you (for whatever reason).

When we say *yes* to our body, we celebrate every curve, every line, every mistaken belief. When we say *yes* there is a shift in Knowing that we are beautiful and perfectly made, a part of the Divine, truly worthy of receiving with favor the divinity of our bodies and spirits. Yes, I love every curve. Yes, I love every dimple—even when it's on my face, or on my butt, or on my thighs. I love every line on my body. I love my Divine self. As of today, I will love the beauty of who I AM. If I have to turn off the television or stop buying magazines that make me feel less because of the false illusions of beauty that society portrays, then so be it. I am Love. I am Divine. I am the essence of Beauty.

We all have moments of darkness when the negative thoughts creep in and weigh us down. One of my friends recently had a baby. She was feeling unattractive and overweight, like she had just lost all of her essence, once she delivered her beautiful little one. Immediately when I heard her voice, I knew something was wrong. I recognized her voice as my own. After all, I have delivered three babies and I felt every punch of emotion that she was expressing.

After reminding her of who she was, I asked her to take the brightest red or black liner and write her "I AM Proclamation" on every mirror in her home.

You, my love, are very important. Every time you brush your teeth, wash your hands, or take a shower, I want you reading those words of truth. Within minutes she sent me a picture of her bathroom mirror with beautiful words of truth boldly displayed. Love, sometimes we have to boldly remind ourselves of our own divine essence to shut off the negative chatter in our minds. After a week she called me and I felt the shift.

It's amazing how words of truth can shine light into our souls and minds to pull us out of dark places. *What is it that you need to say yes to regarding your past or your choices?* Love yourself for where you have been and for what you have learned, even if you have not learned it yet. In the loving yourself, the saying yes to, your freedom arises. Howard Thurman wrote: "To continue one's journey with footsteps guided by the illumination of remembered radiance."

Love, we must arise and do what is needed to walk in that remembered radiance, the time when you were the happiest, or felt beautiful beyond words, or most aligned with that amazing light of God within. This is why we write on our mirrors in our physical homes, and on our hearts and on our minds, so we will remember that which we have always been: Radiant, Beautiful, Love, Joy, and Light. When we remember, others will remember. As I reflected on these exquisite words that Howard Thurman wrote, I also felt that there are times when we cannot remember, just because we have allowed ourselves to become overwhelmed by the circumstances of our hell. I have been face down in the carpet within the closed room of my heart, with no witness, inside my alabaster box, and no one knows the cost.

It is in these moments that we must walk in borrowed remembered radiance. Yes, borrowed. I know you have a person that you admire, that always seems to have it together, someone who life always shines upon with beauty and grace. I want you to borrow that person's radiance and walk in it. Walk in that stunning borrowed radiance until it becomes your own remembered radiance. By borrowing her light, you will be helped through the darkness. In this awareness, I pour my love, my praise, my tears. I pour the beautiful fragrant oil from my alabaster box upon your feet saying, "Arise love and walk in borrowed radiance."

After I wrote this section I was listening to Dr. Wayne Dyer and Dr. Deepak Chopra's presentation "Living Beyond Miracles." Dr. Chopra mentioned a book written by Dr. Ellen Langer called, *Mindfulness*, and the experiment she did with the elderly. Dr. Langer took a number of patients who were eighty years of age and older, and placed them in a 1950s environment for several weeks, instructing them to "Be as you were in the 1950s." Caretakers played Elvis Presley on the radio and the patients watched Alfred Hitchcock on television; books and magazines on the tables were from the 1950s. Life in this secluded environment projected the 1950s which made it easier for the patients to be as they were actually there, living in the 1950s all over again—living in borrowed radiance from an earlier, more youthful time of life.

What happened during this study was quite remarkable! The patients showed signs of reversing biological aging, such as improved hearing, improvements in strength and manual dexterity, and more skin elasticity. So these folks, in their moment of borrowing time or radiance from the1950s, manifested that state in the now. Dr. Chopra reported that once the patients were removed from the 1950s-like environment, they reverted back to their previous state prior to the experiment. Every hair on my body stood up in amazement when I heard this, because I felt the connection immediately. Our minds are so powerful and will manifest what we think we know to be true—lie or fact. The concept of borrowing radiance until you can identify with that which you forgot is a beautiful pathway for stepping back into your personal remembered radiance.

> *It is the feeling of the race that needs to be redeemed and saved from its own self-generated destruction. Until the individual understands the need of Self-control in regard to his feeling – in the waking consciousness – it is impossible to maintain any permanent forward movement of a constructive nature. All accomplishment that is not attained through the Feeling of Divine Love is but temporary, for Divine Love alone is the way to Permanent Perfection.*
> ~*The Magic Presence*, Guy Ballard

This quotation from Guy Ballard explains it even further: when we walk in remembered radiance, we are walking in a time when we felt Divine, Beautiful, Joy, Abundance, Peace, and Love. It is the Feeling separated from the thinking that changes life, us, or our circumstances. This is a manifestation of "fake it until you make it," a concept which holds a lot of truth. If we fake it long enough, then it becomes us, because we have created from a place of desire so strongly that soon enough it is no longer being faked but FELT.

This has worked for me many times. For example, in my employment as a distributor when I would have to learn a new product, or call on a new set of physicians, I felt insecure and not one hundred percent confident, but faking it until I made it always pushed me through. Because it moved me beyond the fear into knowing, which then became my reality because I felt it to be true, or I became comfortable with my new truth.

Today, as we dive in and peel back the layers, understanding the thoughts that have created these barriers, we begin to tear down the walls. This is the beginning of the journey of loving oneself, loving that Radiant Goddess Within. Recognizing that in your acceptance is your freedom, your divine right to love. Writing your proclamation is claiming or officially announcing the amazing things within you that are of great importance. Accept your beauty, your love, your divine inheritance, your Goddess within, and release the rest because you are worthy and it is time.

> *Beauty is a concept different in every mind*
> *Reflecting true values inside*
> *Revealing what is in its purest form*
> *Naturally uncovering and renewing*
> *into something more.*
> *Open your eyes to discover beauty at its best*
> *Look inside yourself*
> *then close your eyes to the rest.*
>
> ~Jenifer Marie

Practicing the I AM

Pick a partner and sit face to face. What do you see with your eyes closed? Each of you takes a turn, reflecting silently on what you see in the other with eyes closed. Then take some time to write down your responses. It is amazing to me what you can see with eyes completely closed. What you see is spirit. When you close your eyes, you stop looking at the flesh and you begin to witness the God in you. Forever Love. Forever Joy. Forever Beautiful. Forever Opulence. Forever Peace. Closing our eyes completely removes the social image we have constructed within ourselves and projected onto others to identify what is beauty or what is not; what we see in the checkout line at the supermarket that permanently taunts our minds. I recently did this activity with my ten-year-old. His response was enlightened and of course he had no idea what his mommy was doing or why. He wrote: "Beautiful, love, and healer." My son was witnessing the Goddess in me and that is what he saw—that which is Forever Beautiful, Joy, Love, Opulence, and Peace. The idea behind this exercise is to start seeing yourself, others, and your world with spiritual eyes that remember radiance, which is God in all things.

When we get to a place of no judgment,
what will we forgive?

~Jenifer Marie

The second step is forgiveness. "Forgiveness" is defined as *the action or process of forgiving, the conscious deliberate decision to release feelings of resentment or vengeance toward a person or a group, who has harmed you.* The words *conscious and deliberate release* resonate with me. It is our decision, our choice, to forgive and let go.

We have to love our selves enough to let go. *What is it that you need to forgive yourself for?* The journey of Love is shining the light of awareness into the dark places of our minds and hearts that have held us back from truly loving ourselves. We have to deliberately be conscious of that which needs to be forgiven and this begins within ourselves. It is facing that negative self-talk that is within our minds and haunts our souls, that we may try to ignore, which needs to be forgiven. Most of what needs to be forgiven are the false illusions that we have created that penalize us internally for things beyond our accountability.

For example, forgiving myself for hating my father as a child. I know hate is a strong word, but prior to my forgiveness, it appropriately describes what I felt. As a child I made myself internally responsible and paid a high price for everything that was apparently wrong with my outer world, and this is what Jenifer needed to forgive. I also needed to forgive myself for not loving me and for being so hard on myself for all these years. I can so easily love my sons unconditionally without reserve, but I can be my own worst enemy, as if I do not deserve the same unconditional love and adoration. In the forgiveness, the resentment toward myself fades away for the light of my own Divinity to prevail.

We must forgive ourselves first, if we are to forgive anyone else and truly be free. This is a master key to the lock that has closed off the soul for lifetimes, which is now to be unlocked. Forgive yourself because you are innocent of all of the false illusions that have pained you, you are right where you are supposed to be, doing exactly what you're supposed to be doing. Everyone has their *ah-ha* moment—hopefully this is yours. Marianne Williams in *A Return to Love*, wrote: "Before the glorious radiance of the kingdom, guilt melts away, and transformed into kindness will nevermore be what it was."

When you forgive yourself, the guilt passes away. You are no longer victim to the pains or choices of the past, and guilt no longer owns you. You are free because you choose to forgive, you choose to love. In that choosing, in that forgiveness, is a kindness that is beyond words beautiful and picturesque, your heaven on Earth. Once you forgive yourself, the shift will heal your heart, and you will never again return to that place of pain and suffering. From this moment on, you recognize that you are a spiritual being having a human experience in this school of life; going higher with each awareness; accepting and loving and forgiving daily.

Unless a discord is forgotten, it is not forgiven, because you cannot lose it or release yourself from it until it is out of your consciousness. So long as you remember an injustice or a disturbed feeling, you have not forgiven the person or the condition.

~*The Magic Presence,* Guy Ballard

It is remembering the details, the painful feelings, that keep the condition alive and unforgiven, and give the person or condition power over your mind and life. In order to truly forgive ourselves, we must forget what we "thought" we did wrong and never bring it back up again, which is true forgiveness. The lesson of forgiveness is so powerful because it is what holds us back from loving ourselves, loving others, and creates the negative patterns in our lives that cause misery and suffering. If we are bound by an unforgiven past, then how are we to have a free and loving future? We can choose to be our own biggest fan or our own worst enemy, by simply forgiving or not. We have free will and dominion over our lives and our minds.

Ask yourself the following questions: *What is it that I need to forgive myself for? Why? What is preventing me from forgiving myself? What barriers have I put up to prevent myself from being that from which I AM? How can I forgive myself and forget so I will never bring it up again?*

The negative chatter inside our minds will shift as we shine the light of truth into our own garden of our hearts and minds. Love, you are worth the power of your own forgiveness. When we get to a place of no judgment, what will we forgive? Let's define that place where we can just be without justification, and allow life to be, and people to be— free and loving, no right or wrong: Love Living Life.

> *Love is life's longing for itself*
> *Whispers across time to awaken the soul*
> *Divine beauty arising from deep within*
> *To ignite the flame of God's light*
> *For it never to go out again*
>
> ~Jenifer Marie

The third step is to recognize our own worthiness. Love, it is time to let go of the unworthiness. "Worthy" is defined as *good, deserving respect, praise or attention; having enough good qualities to be considered important or useful.* I want to recognize the divine qualities within that say I AM good enough and important enough to be love. During a challenging experience in my life, I received a phone call from my domestic violence counselor, strongly advising me to take the kids and go to a safe house. I told her I would pray about it but had no intention of running. The entire day, I just kept replaying her words, *"He knows your routine; your life is in danger."* As I prayed and cried and denied, I realized that I could not be stubborn and put my children in danger. So I packed our bags as if we were going on vacation and had a friend drop us off along a long dark driveway. I had my little one on my hip and four other little feet behind me dragging their suitcases.

The safe house was in a normal subdivision with privacy, only with extreme security, which meant that someone was awake and watching cameras/motion detectors at all times. I checked us in and I remember feeling like I didn't belong there. I wondered why this was happening to me. Indeed, the several weeks that we were there seemed surreal. I wore wigs out in public, swapped cars every other day, had different people pick up the boys from school. My life had changed dramatically just for the sake of saving it.

The women that came in daily had broken limbs or bruises on their bodies and faces; our broken-ness was the same even though it looked completely different. Daily after all the children were in bed, the women were assigned rooms to clean, which included mopping, dusting, and sterilizing. After we were done, I would sit at the kitchen table with the other women and we would share our stories—always going back to God. I had pulled out my Bible one night and was sharing the story of Judas; more importantly explaining the significance of thanking our own personal Judas (more on this in the next chapter).

There was one woman off in the corner, quiet with her pain and suffering. I invited her to join us and she said, "I cannot because I do not believe as you believe; I am a Buddhist." Well, thank God I had been studying different religions and the connections between them. I guess the Universe knew I would need that understanding. The next words out of my mouth to her were: "I am a Buddhist too!" She looked at me with surprise, as did all the other women at the table, because she knew I had a Bible in my hand and was speaking about God. I looked at her and asked her if she knew the definition of the word "Buddhist"? I told her that Buddhist means *enlightened one*. That everyone who has a higher awareness is enlightened.

From that conversation, she began to join our women's group of healing. She told us her story. She was eight months pregnant with her first child. Her husband was the son of a preacher. She and her husband were in church every time the doors were open. He would raise his hands in church to praise God and raise his hands to beat her the rest of the time. The last beating almost killed her and her baby. He was in jail and she was finally safe. She had projected her pain and hurt upon God, instead of recognizing it was her husband's issues.

Several weeks after leaving the safe house, she called me, overwhelmed with joy. I thought she had had the baby. Her excitement was not from delivering her baby though, she was still very pregnant, but from buying her first Bible. As tears flowed down my face, I realized my purpose in that safe house wasn't just for me but was for her and those beautiful women that may have heard the truth. Those beautiful women that needed to release and forgive. Those women who needed someone to say, *"Don't go back; you are worth so much more. You are worthy. You do not deserve to be mistreated. You are not your pain or the actions of others. You are Love. You are Divine. You are most important and you are Worthy."*

The journey of Love begins the moment we recognize the I AM within ourselves that says I am worthy, I am love, I am beautiful, I am enough. I thank God for this realization and for the experience of truth. How much of my life have I failed to notice when someone else needed help, missing the opportunity because I did not have the eyes to see? What will it take for us to recognize that we are worthy, and beautiful, and whole— nothing missing, nothing broken?

In recognizing who you are is a knowing that you are completely worthy of love in all its beauty. Acceptance, forgiveness, and recognizing worthiness leads us to the I AM proclamation. I want you to write in your Journal of One: I AM….then let the words flow without judgment. As we continue to grow together, meditate, and plant positive seeds in our garden, the shift will manifest. You must do the work. It took years or maybe several lifetimes to create the barriers; it will take your intention, more than one day, or one journal entry, to bring down the walls. Your willingness to ask the questions and answer honestly is the beginning of the process.

Today I choose to love the Goddess within

I will place my Divine crown back upon my head

Never to take it off again

I will remind myself daily that beauty and radiance shine from within

and that God made me in perfection, just as I AM

Today, I will let go of all the false illusions that create negativity in my mind

and I will smile and send positive energy to the world just to remind

That we were created in the image of LOVE in this fraction of time

To heal ourselves…to heal the world…

and to manifest the Goddess Divine.

~Jenifer Marie

Meditative Journaling — Chapter 2

1. **What patterns in my past have created barriers against Love?**
2. **What is it within myself that I need to say YES to?**
3. **What is preventing me from forgiving myself and why?**
4. **What do I need to accept to walk in my worthiness and Divine Love?**

Chapter 3

Thanking My Judas

How can we truly forgive the ones who have hurt us? If love is our most important life lesson, then forgiveness would be the second. It is so easy to identify with the victim mentality to justify life or current situations that are painful or not what we want them to be. To refuse to forgive is an unconscious excuse to continue with the old patterns that create fertile ground for suffering. It is so easy to keep pointing and blaming outside of ourselves, rather than standing up to own the truth. In the standing up, the owning, is a recognition that some part of ourselves brought us here, in this moment, to grow through the current situation.

Through all of my trials, I have found myself in a deep search for truth and solitude. I have studied different religions and beliefs, and found inspiration anywhere I could find the words. During a difficult time in my life, my aunt and spiritual teacher came to stay with me for awhile. She told me once after a challenging day, "Jen, you need to learn to thank your Judas." Later that evening after our deep discussion, I began to read about Judas and apply this concept to my current situation. You may or may not be familiar with the story of Judas, but he was one of the twelve disciples, who betrayed Jesus by turning him in to the priests for thirty silver coins. This happened in the garden of Gethsemane, which is found on the lower slope of the Mount of Olives, in Jerusalem. Judas led the army to Jesus, with the agreement that they would arrest the man he kissed.

Here is the revelation: If Judas had not turned in Jesus, there would not have been a crucifixion, and none of us would be free. Judas was doing exactly what he was supposed to be doing. In this knowing, I realized we all have our own Judas. Each of us has been kissed, betrayed, and crucified. In my awareness, I realized that we must thank our Judas to truly release and forgive. If we understand that our Judas is doing exactly what he or she is supposed to, which is to take us higher in our consciousness, then how can we not forgive? In the forgiveness, in the thanking, you are releasing. *Who is your Judas? Who has kissed you while betraying you? Who has crucified you so that you could be free and go higher? If Jesus could love Judas right where he was at with his knowing, then who am I to be any different?* I had to learn to thank my Judas and I didn't just thank him once. I continuously thanked him. Even to this day, if I forget, I thank him again. My love, thank your Judas and recognize the lessons, the gifts that come from the hurt.

> *Unless a discord is forgotten, it is not forgiven, because you cannot lose it or release yourself from it until it is out of your consciousness. So long as you remember an injustice or a disturbed feeling, you have not forgiven the person or the condition.*
>
> ~*The Magic Presence,* Guy Ballard

I offer this quote again to highlight how important it is for us to forget perceived transgressions against us to truly forgive. This is where most of us get stuck. We think we have forgiven, we have cut the tethers, done our spiritual prayers for release, but my God-ness how the thoughts of the injustice keep surfacing, which means we really have not forgiven at all. We just put a bandage on our wound; but we still have it to lean in and reflect, to create even more forgiveness in our lives. You may be tethered by things and not even recognize why. For years this was me—I was still in victim mode unconsciously and telling my story, *How can you forgive someone who wanted to destroy you?* Who was I serving by hanging on and not forgiving? My ego, my past, or my future? I was serving fear still by hanging on to my un-forgiveness and unconsciously creating more of the same negative patterns in my life. It is the remembering of the details, the painful feelings, that keep the conditions alive and unforgiven, and give the person or condition power over your mind and life.

I would like to share with you a powerful mental exercise that I read in *The Book of Love and Creation* by Paul Selig. In this mental exercise, you make a list of all of the ones who have hurt you. You imagine that you are on a riverbank and you release each person that is on your list into the river with blessings. The idea is to bless them for the lessons and then release them to love to take back your power. The last person you release is yourself. This is such a powerful exercise. I actually read this process and re-read it again and again. Doing this process was such a powerful experience. I literally felt the release. I closed my eyes and I saw my father, my mother, friends, ex-husbands, ex-lovers, even my children. I wrote in my journal a list of everyone I might need to forgive. I had an entire page and guess who was number one? MYSELF. I went and purchased leather tethers and created my own ceremony of cutting my chains—releasing the negative, thanking each one, and blessing them beyond words. Here is my journal entry after I completed this mental exercise:

> As I released the un-forgiveness....I felt the Divine Love rush over me. I felt my energy increase. My vibration is higher. We don't realize how un-forgiveness holds us back. The visualization from The Book of Love and Creation is a tool that will bless and heal many. It is not enough to just thank your Judas. You have to bless them, release, bless, and visualize the divine river of love/life washing over them, returning them to the source. In doing this, we recognize the lessons that were meant to come forth. We un-tether, un-bound, and release that which frees our beautiful spirits to love by Divinity. To see the world with the eyes of God. On this journey of One...forgiveness is a key step toward "whole"ness. To fulfill our higher purpose and to go higher together. The powerful river of Divine Love washes and makes anew. The un-forgiveness that I once held in my heart released—free to go back to the source. My entire being relaxed, at peace. As if every one of my cells in my body is smiling and screaming "thank you." As I released, I saw the lessons, I felt my Truth, and I recognized the purpose of all my Judas. The power forgiveness has is beyond words. Un-forgiveness has the power to cripple and hold us back from fulfilling our life purpose. Forgiveness has the magnificent power to heal the world. Either way...it is our Choice. I choose to heal. I choose to release. I choose to thank my Judas! I choose to see with the eyes of God. I choose to Love. As I choose, I heal the world.

As you can see and feel from my journal entry, I took back my power. That is the gift I would like to give to you. Take back your power from those things that have bound you and held you back from Love. How can you take back your power? The mental exercise is a great start, but it has to happen within a powerful manifestation. As I was praying about this chapter, I thought, *How did Jesus forgive?* The answer came immediately. The three aspects of forgiving our Judas are: take nothing personally, let go of right or wrong, and have no expectations.

Taking nothing personally means you are willing to sit back and recognize it is not about you. This can be a challenge because from the time we could speak we said *mine* and started to create our worlds as such. So how do we begin to move our lives from a personal to an impersonal space? One way is to recognize that we are not our bodies, not this flesh. Just to shift perspective and to realize that we are spiritual beings, not human beings, this can help open our eyes, increase our awareness. This is a powerful step toward living the I AM.

Another way to forgive and be in the impersonal position is to let go of right and wrong. When we live life personally, we identify and relate to our world through our thoughts and experiences, which causes a victim mentality and creates poison. Ego is connected to right and wrong and keeps us living life personally. When we live life impersonally, we identify with our source, the life energy that flows from within. This begins the shift from living from the mind to living from the heart, which is our highest nature.

The final step to forgiveness is to have no expectations. If someone has hurt us or we have perceived we've been wronged, then our expectations about next steps will keep us locked into the past and pain. Letting go of our expectations means the person may never apologize, may never even recognize they did anything wrong. Letting go of expectations means that you are not going to get revenge. We all have heard *an eye for an eye* but when we truly forgive, we must release the idea of getting even or payback. Remember the three aspects of forgiveness: nothing personal, letting go of right and wrong, and no expectations equal no judgment.

> *When we get to a place of no judgment,*
> *what will we forgive?*
>
> ~Jenifer Marie

It is your choice. I choose Love. I choose to forgive. I choose to thank my Judas.

Meditative Journaling — Chapter 3

1. **Who is my Judas and what have I learned?**
2. **Make a list of all the people you need to forgive.**
3. **How am I going to use the three aspects of forgiveness to release and heal?**

Chapter 4

The Seeds of the Mind Grow in the Garden of Your Soul

Open your mind to imagine
your heart free from lies
The power of manipulation
controlling the mind
Molding you into someone
you are not
Only to wake up in a "state of
I forgot"
Searching to seek the One
lost long ago
Only to find a better
version of oneself
without the ego.

~Jenifer Marie

As I sit alone in this room, darkness surrounds me. It's as if my eyes are closed, but they are open and I can't see. In the darkness, I look for the light. The mind begins to replay the same scenes, which create fear. *Am I safe? I can't see what is in front of me.*

All of the movies and images we have taken in begin to create our story or take away from it. *Am I enough? Pretty enough? Thin enough? Successful enough?* All we see are images of beauty that society paints for us: on television, in magazines, and on the Internet. In this dark room the negative self-talk continues. I hear the chatter.

I sit up in my chair and hold my hand in front of my face, still unable to see, but knowing my hand is in front of me. In an instant, a small flicker of light (awareness) penetrates the dark. I begin to see, minimally, that the room is safe. My light increases in brightness. I inhale deeply knowing all is well and exhale slowly. As the room comes to life with light, I see a mirror before me. For the first time, I see me. I see the divine beauty of this vessel. I see the pure essence of spirit, which illuminates from within and shines outward. I see me and I see all in the same divine light, awakening from the dark. It is when the light comes on that you realize that all along the light switch was within reach. All that we have ever searched for is within.

If you were to think of your mind as a garden, then you would be more guarded of the seeds (thoughts) you planted. I think we all can agree that what we think, we manifest. I would like to take this concept a little deeper. Everything in our environment that we are exposed too, impacts our thoughts. Now there are things beyond our realm of control—namely we cannot control others.

The Seeds of the Mind Grow in the Garden of Your Soul 49

But we can control what we think and how we respond to others. Each of us is accountable and responsible for our own thoughts; for they become our heaven or our hell. My question for you is this: *What are you taking in that influences your thoughts?* Your thoughts are your seeds. Your mind is your soil. Your garden is where your seeds grow and reality manifests.

For me, the shift took place on 9/11. I was ironing my clothes, preparing for a modeling job when the images came across the television screen. I stood in complete shock and disbelief, unable to even understand why. My heart was broken and I expected life to stop for at least one day so I could mourn. I called the modeling company to confirm cancellation due to events, but was completely surprised to find out the shoot was still on schedule. For the next several weeks, I was consumed by the news, the devastation, the sorrow, and the heartache. Fear began to just consume me. All I wanted to do was to make the pain go away for so many who were suffering, but I had no way to accomplish this.

This was one of my *ah-ha* moments, when a shift took place within me. I recognized that I could continue to take in the devastation, manifesting depression within me for things I couldn't control. I decided to turn off the television, which turned off the images replaying in my mind. Remember when the light comes on, the picture changes. Turning my physical television off shifted my intellectual/emotional television. I stopped planting seeds of fear. I stopped planting seeds of sadness and sorrow. I began to shift and plant seeds of love to help all of those who were hurting and to help myself. This is when my garden changed. This is when my light came on and I began my journey into consciousness.

The darkness represents lack of knowledge. The only way to

shift is to align to a new truth (light), your truth, and go higher. The only way this shift can manifest is to recognize that you are a spiritual being having a physical experience. In that knowing, you are powerful, and a part of the Divine. In that knowing you are creating a heaven (or a hell, which is a present reality). As one thinks and feels, so life is. In this understanding, we recognize that thoughts shape our reality, but how we feel is the gateway to our heaven or hell. As we awaken to our true nature, mastering our thoughts and emotions will shape reality. If we want to change the world, then it starts within the heart.

As one thinks and feels, so life is. I posted this thought on Facebook with a photo of a lake with a beautiful mirror image of clouds. The only reflection seen was what was above. We are projecting our reality out of what we think and feel, which is truth. If we planted a spring garden with tomatoes, squash, and cucumbers, then when it came time to harvest and we had lemons, beets, and zucchini, I think we would question the obvious. This should be the same for our lives. The shift will come once we realize we are planting the seeds in our minds by what we think and feel, which impacts our reality.

There are several things we can do to change the seeds or choose differently. One is to avoid negativity. Negativity breeds more negativity. I often share with others that I have a "see no evil, hear no evil, speak no evil" Buddha statue, which serves as the perfect illustration of the state of mind where we choose the positive. We are the masters of our own minds and where we choose to focus our attention will create our thoughts and feelings. If you do not currently like the circumstances or state of your mind, then look at your thoughts and your attention to find the cause. Once you identify your thoughts and feelings, then you can begin to be more conscious of what you are focusing on and the shift will begin. We live in a world that is full of negativity and violence, but focusing on the negativity and violence only breeds more negativity and violence. Who is to blame? Who is accountable? If everyone would focus on love, then how would our world be different? As you awaken to this truth, the world will awaken. It begins within you.

Another way you can improve or change the seeds being planted in your mind is to only take in what you want to manifest. If you want more joy in your world, then focus your attention and thoughts on things that bring you joy. If you want more love in your world, then focus on what brings you love and BE that. If you want more peace in your world, then focus your attention on things that bring your heart peace and BE that. Where your attention goes, your energy flows, and you manifest. Uncontrolled or unmastered thoughts only mold you and your world into someone and something you are not. Once you recognize the essence of who you are, then you begin to awaken and realize that you have been living in a state of forgetfulness.

> *Summing it all up friends, I'd say you'll do best by filling your minds and meditating on things true, noble, reputable, authentic, compelling, gracious—the best, not the worst; the beautiful, not the ugly; things to praise and not things to curse. Put into practice what you learned from me, what you heard and saw and realized. Do that and God, who makes everything work together, will work you into his most excellent harmonies.*
>
> ~Phil 4:8-9, *The Message Bible*

Meditative Journaling — Chapter 4

1. How have my thoughts and feelings impacted my current reality?

2. What needs to change so I can plant different seeds in my mind?

3. How would my life be better if I focused on what I desire?

Chapter 5

The Journey Out of Fear

And the moment came when she stood at the edge of life, trusted her cape of faith, and jumped!

~Journal entry, Jenifer Marie

We're all hallucinating. And that's what the world is: a mass hallucination where fear seems more real than love. Fear is an illusion. Our craziness, paranoia, anxiety and trauma are literally all imagined.

~Marianne Williamson, *A Return to Love: Reflections on the Principles of A Course in Miracles*

One afternoon my oldest son, Nik, took his brother, Cameron, to a nature preserve to spend some time together. During their hike, they both decided to climb a tree— apparently my oldest had climbed this particular tree many times before, whereas my youngest does not usually like climbing at all. So my oldest climbed up to the top with ease (at least that was his explanation of events) and my youngest attempted to follow behind him. During his climb, Cameron froze, pressed his forehead against the bark of the tree, and with his ears turning blood red, he began to yell out loud, "Oh God, I need Help!" My oldest, looking down on his brother, began to laugh, even as Cameron was sincerely yelling for help. At this point Nik instructed him to just jump. Although he was close enough to the ground to jump, in his mind my youngest son felt like he was up ten feet high and in danger. These feelings initiated his response and for him were valid. But in reality, he was maybe one or two feet from the ground and was in no danger at all.

When they came home and told me the story, we all laughed out loud, not at my youngest but with him. (Since then, if we need to laugh, say on a Monday morning when we need to get out of bed for school, we just recount the story.) This anecdote illustrates quite nicely that perception is everything and fear is an illusion in our minds.

"Fear" is defined as *an illusion, feelings of anxiety, an unpleasant emotion caused by the belief that someone or something is dangerous, or a response to a perceived threat that is consciously recognized as danger, which stimulates the fight or flight response.* What is it that we are truly afraid of? I'm not talking about phobic fears, such as heights, snakes, or spiders. I want to go a lot deeper than that. Another definition of fear is *separation from God.* As soon as I read that definition I said out loud, *"Anything that creates fear separates us from our true selves, the Divine within, which then causes more separation and creates more fear."*

Fear of Love

Love is what we were born with. Fear is what we have learned here. The spiritual journey is the relinquishment—or unlearning—of fear and the acceptance of love back into our hearts.—Marianne

Williamson, *A Return to Love: Reflections on the Principles of a Course in Miracles*

All of my life, I have accepted God into my heart, under the impression that by doing so I would be saved and go to heaven. It has taken me over twenty-five years to recognize that I have to let go of fear to truly accept Love, which is God, into my heart. I am currently reading Marianne Williamson's book, *A Return to Love: Reflections on the Principles of a Course in Miracles*. I am in awe at how aligned spirit is and how we truly are so connected. The words that I read are a reflection of what I have already written and know to be true— which is beautiful. What I know to be true is that love is what we are born with; and I have experienced that fear is what shadows the true essence of the Divine self. Fear can keep us from loving ourselves and from receiving the love of another. Our minds, or fear, are so powerful, we can talk ourselves out of a good thing. All because we do not want to repeat the past, so we transfer the pain and the fear from relationship to relationship. Overcoming the fear that is learned is part of our spiritual journey to truly love ourselves and to receive love. One of my greatest lessons has been to let go of the fear of being loved and to release the fear that the love I knew in the past was going to repeat. I had to learn to say *yes* to life loving me exactly as I have always deserved, which included a healthy loving relationship with myself and with another.

It was December 2015, and an advertisement for Intuitive Healing Massage caught my attention. I love to get a massage—but to have a healing session during a massage was appealing and had to be exactly what I needed. Life had been overwhelming. Work was pulling me in different directions. Christmas shopping and activities and planning and decorating the house were exhausting me. Emotionally, I had undergone some major family changes that had taken a powerful toll on my spirit that meditation alone could not shake.

Because one of my sons was having a difficult time, I was not only hurting for him, but I was also questioning my idea of who I was as a mother. I had to let go of the concept that I could save my son. This warrior mom in me that has always fought the good fight had to surrender and die another death of illusion. It had been a three year struggle to help guide my son back on the right path and I finally found myself up against a wall. At that point I had no choice but to let go. He had to go live with his dad and I had to be okay with that decision. I thought by holding on tighter, I could be what he needed, but it was actually in the letting go that gave him his greatest opportunity for healing. In the letting go, my heart was broken wide open in a way that I have never experienced, which had taxed me spiritually and physically. I thought perhaps that ancient healing techniques to balance mind, body, and spirit would harmonize this depleted vessel. So, I made an appointment, with the highest anticipation that something magical was going to happen, or at least I would get a ninety minute nap with a massage.

I laid on the table face down, under the cover, and immediately fell into a deep relaxed state. I had a feeling of peace and I silently gave the masseuse permission "in," to align me and release the negative, which no longer served me. She came into the room and my session began. This experience was different because the masseuse spoke during the entire massage—revealing insights or anything that needed to be cleared. As she continued, I felt my way through her words to hear my worth. In a moment she paused and asked me, "What is it that you are so afraid of? What are you so worried about? Why don't you let him love you?" I lifted my head from the face down position, despite the heaviness of my relaxed state, and I looked up in surprise. Nothing spoken—only felt—as my eyes looked at hers.

I hadn't seen that coming, out of everything that I interpreted to be currently blocking my flow of life, I hadn't thought that letting a man love me was one of the reasons my mind, body, and spirit were out of balance—or maybe it was. *I said yes to dinner but did I say yes to love? He is an amazing man, treats me like I have never been treated, loves me beyond words, and loves my boys; so what was my problem?* I had no idea until that moment, when I felt her words pierce my heart, that I had walls around my heart like the Great Wall of China and no one was getting through. Even after all of the time alone, releasing, and healing, I was still holding back, but completely oblivious about it. My ego was still dominating my life, even though I thought I had released and unlearned to get to a place where I could write a book about overcoming "life lessons." The biggest life lesson of all is that we are continuously learning and that never changes!

I turned face down again, my heart swelled with emotion and the masseuse said, "Give that little girl a lollipop and send her on her way!!!" Unbelievable, the little girl is there still, even after all this time, kicking and silently holding me back behind the curtain of my life. In that moment, because I said yes to the clearing and healing, I felt the release. And I did—emotionally, spiritually, and physically—give that little girl a lollipop and sent her on her way. The fear of love prevents us from truly loving ourselves and places unconscious protective barriers that prevent us from truly being loved by another. That is our safety net, the fear of love which creates the separation from ourselves and anyone who truly loves us, delivering the false illusion of safety. The fear of love creates the patterns that we unconsciously do not realize we have created, but continues to place us in the illusion of suffering.

> *Then the moment came when she realized the love*
> *she sought in another was within and silently loving*
> *herself all along.*
>
> ~Jenifer Marie

The fear of love also keeps us looking outside of ourselves for that one special person or Mr. Right; the one who will complete us and make all this pain go away. The reality is that all we need is within us, and once we recognize who we are, then we can understand that the fear of love is an illusion created by us in our minds to keep us separate from God, from ourselves and Love. Marianne Williamson, in *A Course in Miracles*, describes this perfectly by categorizing our relationships as holy or unholy, as follows:

> *For an unholy relationship is based on differences, where each one thinks the other has what he has not. They come together, each to complete himself and rob the other. They stay until they think that there is nothing left to steal, and then move on. And so they wander through a world of strangers, unlike themselves, living with their bodies perhaps under a common roof that shelters neither, in the same room and yet a world apart.*

A holy relationship starts from a different premise.
Each one has looked within and seen no lack.
Accepting his completion, he would extend it by
joining with another, whole as himself.

This is a perfect description of how my relationships have been in the past, based on fear, differences, and seeking to find "out there" instead of recognizing that I have all that I need within me. After reading this, I researched the word "holy." One definition of holy is *set apart for the service of God*, which is beautiful beyond words and describes each and every one of us, whether we recognize it or not. Some synonyms for holy are *sacred*, *divine*, and *blessed*, which also describe each and every one of us. In Hebrew, holy is "qodesh", which means set-apartness. In the New Testament, holy is "hagios," which means *set apart, sacred*, and *worthy of veneration* (great respect). A fear of love begins with not recognizing that we are holy, which is a knowing that we are set apart and sacred and worthy of loving the Goddess within prior to loving another person. This is the first level of awareness that must be accepted so we can create holy relationships and stop the negative patterns of repeating unholy relationships, which causes us more pain and suffering.

The shift in awareness focuses on our internal/eternal fountain of unconditional love—God—within us that sustains and nourishes beyond anything in this world. The moment we can have this holy encounter or holy awareness of ourselves is the moment when we can truly begin to create holy relationships based on love and not lack or need. This is letting go of the fear of love by recognizing that you are holy and deserve to receive the highest respect, in this moment, this life, now. Love, we no longer look outside of ourselves for someone to make us happy, or love us in the right way, because in this moment we accept our own responsibility that we are set apart for such a time as this to be holy, to be love, to be peace and to create from that Being, which is God and not fear.

I had to love myself completely to let go of the fear of Love and choose to let Love in. I had to decide to love myself with all of the desire that I have ever wanted from another. It was time and there was no more hiding. The Goddess within is worthy and beautiful and had been waiting lifetimes for me to decide to Love myself completely. Again and again and again, I say, I choose love.

The first step in the journey out of fear is letting go of the fear of love. Already, we have focused in great detail on loving ourselves, but beyond all of what we know is an intense fear of loving another. We are afraid to love, literally terrified. We are afraid to completely surrender to love for the fear of being hurt. As we grow from infancy and take in this world with our carnal eyes, all we see are images of pain associated with love, which manifest in our world to become our reality. I can assure you that I am no expert on love, but it is the lessons we all learn that make each of us go higher in our consciousness, which leads back to one powerful statement: there is no fear in love. In not knowing, how can we claim to love when we are consumed by fear?

All the wisdom books I have read, from the Bible to *The Mastery of Love* by Miguel Ruiz, reveal there is no fear in love. In *The Mastery of Love*, there is a beautiful story of a man and a woman who did not believe in love because of what they had perceived love to be. With this belief, they owned responsibility for their own happiness and worth, not looking outside themselves for validation. In spite of this presumption that love didn't exist, they began to unconsciously fall in love with each other.

This is the day, which we have all experienced, when something inside our minds lies and says my happiness, love, and peace are because of another person. The moment the man placed his happiness, his love, in the hands of another, disappointment and heartbreak manifested. No one outside of ourselves can truly make us happy. This is a perfect example of an "unholy relationship," that which focuses on someone or something outside of ourselves to make us happy or complete. Your joy, your love, your beauty is this indescribable essence that is within you, as in me. In love, most of us look outside of ourselves for someone else to love me, validate me, and make me happy—perhaps the majority of relationships are based on these concepts. But the moment we look in the mirror and take responsibility for our own happiness, our own love, the shift happens.

At what point do we stop blaming others for things that have been done, which we believe were wrong? At what point do we stop being the victim of past choices and relationships that have permanently poisoned our hearts. We need to get to that place where we no longer bleed unconsciously with toxic intentions into every aspect of our lives, especially our relationships; that place where the knowing is revealed, and awareness has made her beautiful presence known. We step into that holy encounter that recognizes who we are, how we love, and how we give, to create beauty within and all around us. In this moment, the light shines upon the shadow that has taunted every aspect of our relationships in the past. With positive intentions and knowing beyond all knowing, we rise up in love and we choose to love ourselves with all the essence of our consciousness, a holy encounter.

As I reflect back on my previous relationships, I know I have done all of the above, expecting my partners to make me happy—placing my star into their hands. As a matter of fact, I have placed my star in the hands of others in all my relationships—with family, friends, and even my children. Remember that everyone in our lives is here for a reason, doing exactly what they are supposed to be doing, saying exactly what they are supposed to be saying, and everyone has an *ah-ha* moment. It takes honest self-reflection to identify the unconscious intentions that may have contributed to the loss of love or relationships. This is a quote I wrote in one of my journal entries:

She realized no love from another could save her... only the Divine love of her self could take her out of fear.

~Jenifer Marie

The moment we recognize who we are, Holy, our Divinity, which takes us back to loving ourselves, the accountability changes, the shift manifests, and you are freed from the fear of love. So give that little girl a lollipop and send her on her way because you were created in love, for love, to create love for all who witness your beauty.

FEAR OF DEATH

"Fear is only as deep as the mind allows."

~Japanese Proverb

The fear of death is probably one of the greatest fears among many, but perhaps the least discussed. We are so afraid of dying that even talking about it makes most of us uncomfortable. *Why do we fear death in the first place? How do we overcome the fear of death? Can we overcome it by being receptive in the right moment in time and yielding to the divine opportunity?* I believe so. I am sharing only to help others, not to disrespect any religious view or anyone's belief. Religion is necessary for many, for some it is the only way to perceive their truth for this lifetime. There is truth in all belief; however, I want to share a different perspective on truth in hopes it will alleviate your fear of transcending.

Like many, I grew up in a household where we went to church, and I was taught beliefs which I didn't question, from southern Baptist to Pentecostal. The one constant that I was conditioned to believe was: You get one life and when you die you go to heaven or hell. So I would pray for forgiveness weekly and hope beyond all hope that I would get to go to heaven. The praying alone did not take away the fear though; underneath it all I was wondering, *Will I be forgiven?* As a child, even though I was innocent, I was completely overwhelmed by this enormous fear of not going to heaven. I remember being afraid of the thought of dying, but being too young to question the dogma I had been given. Even as an adult, in all of my self study, I never questioned my beliefs regarding reincarnation or death, it just silently was there all along, like a make believe childhood friend that never leaves your side, or mind.

Until one day I came across a book that flipped my table over and created an *ah-ha* moment: *Many Lives, Many Masters* by Dr. Brian Weiss. At this time in my life, I was selling a sleep medication to psychiatrists, so I was drawn to read any book written by a psychiatrist. (Just a quick disclosure, it is very intimidating to call on a doctor, a psychiatrist, that can read you and analyze you, while you're trying to help their patients. This is why I wanted to read anything written by psychiatrists so I could begin to understand their way of thinking.)

So I began reading *Many Lives, Many Masters* by Dr. Brian Weiss. I could not put the book down! I read the entire book in one day! Every single word resonated with my inner being in such a way that I knew it was truth, which opened my eyes to a bigger truth: we do not live just one life. So this book has now shifted my thoughts and created fertile ground for me to question the creed, the belief I was raised with, to find my own truth, maybe somewhere in the middle. I found myself in a sacred place within, questioning and listening intently. If I believe in an all powerful, mighty, loving, glorious God, that created this beautiful realm in which in my eyes delight, then why would I believe without question that He could not re-create me again to learn what I am supposed to learn, especially knowing how hard-headed I can be? Surely it will take more than one life for me to listen and learn and know beyond all knowing, to fulfill my purpose—this I know as truth. If you haven't read the book, *Many Lives, Many Masters*, then I do not want to give it away, but for any book to draw me in so tightly that I would miss sleep (very important to this sleep diva), food, and extra time at night with my children, it has to be amazing.

This was my catalyst to allow me to re-think or think for the first time; and even to listen to that still small voice inside that I know is truth, to understand death on a deeper level, which in turn helped me to embrace the lessons of this life. But that is how spirit works, it just takes one thing to grab your attention, open your eyes, to let light into your mind, into the dark space that has been stagnant for years with pain and suffering. Thank God for the *ah-ha* moments, which have humbly brought me here writing these words for you. I use the analogy that I was in a religious box for years with the lid on tight, suffocating and gasping for air, life, or just more. Until one day I took the lid off and stood on top of the box, literally screaming in freedom just for the release of all the negative, invited or not, taught or taken, regardless, the release was enormous.

This is how I released the fear of death, by being hungry enough for truth, presented to me in the perfect moment of receptivity, and I began to question, discover, hear, feel, and know. It was my knowing beyond all knowing that changed everything. Now if the opportunity arises and life presents someone that is ready for the shift, I will ask: "How many people do you know that are going to make it off of this earth alive?" Not one person. But we silently live our entire lives in fear, anticipating the unexpected moment, which we each have to face alone: death. My next question is always: "If you knew you could come back again, with the same loved ones, different titles, different roles, maybe even different ethnicities, then would it make the fear of death dissipate?"

> *Most people are so afraid of living because they just might die and most are afraid of dying because they have not lived.*
>
> ~Jenifer Marie

When I wrote those lines I literally laughed from my head to my toes; so true that fear captivates us enough to keep us from fully living; and even as we exhale our last breath fear still reigns, unless we choose otherwise. But why? Why does the fear of death consume us to the point that we do not comprehend or attempt to understand concepts that could truly set us free? It is the unknowing that frightens us beyond words.

I went to a Hay House workshop and witnessed a live presentation by Anita Moorjani, author of *Dying to Be Me: My Journal from Cancer, to Near Death, to True Healing*, speak about her near death experience. Moorjani described her experience saying, "…and then I was overwhelmed by the realization that God isn't a being, but a state of Being and I was now that state of being." She also described crossing over as being "totally engulfed in love."

When she spoke about her experience there was no sadness or pain, but rather this indescribable love that she experienced with an expanded awareness of her life's truths, which became evidently clear in that moment. Her words magnificently described her experience and how she understood life now in a completely different light, a light of love and a present heaven. If this is death, then why do we fear it with every fiber of our being?

> *By knowledge we approach God.*
>
> ~*Many Lives, Many Masters*, Dr. Brian L. Weiss

Fear of Life

Our deepest fear is not that we are inadequate. Our deepest fear is that we are powerful beyond measure. It is our light, not our darkness that frightens us. We ask ourselves, "Who am I to be brilliant, gorgeous, talented, fabulous?" Actually, who are you not to be? You are a child of God. Your playing small does not serve the world. There is nothing enlightened about shrinking so that other people won't feel insecure around you. We are all meant to shine, as children do. We were born to make manifest the glory of God that is within us. It is not just in some of us; it is in everyone. And as we let our own light shine, we unconsciously give other people permission to do the same. As we are liberated from our own fear, our presence automatically liberates others.

~Marianne Williamson, *A Return To Love*

As we release ourselves from our own fear, we give others permission to do the same, to live a life without fear. Why do we fear life at all? I believe we are afraid of not being enough and being too much— the paradox of polar opposites—and it is the place somewhere in the middle that keeps us safe, in our comfort zone. As Williamson states, we are not here to be small, that is not why God created us, but we spend our whole lives trying to figure out who we are, why we came, which is remembering everything we forgot from the very beginning. It is the unlearning or un-conditioning of the mind to remember that we are the manifestation of the I AM and we are meant to do amazing things; all of us. The confusion is this: if we stay small, it is comfortable, stable, and secure because we don't want change and we want to feel safe.

We want to know beyond all knowing that the job is going to be there, the lights are going to come on when we flip the switch, food is in the refrigerator, and the calendar of events is planned, completely aware of what to expect and when, only then can we pretend we are not afraid. So we become stuck in jobs we hate, with unmet desires, and life seems to fall short —all because we are afraid to step outside the line of what we know. Until life presents itself in an unexpected moment. Then the choice is available loud and clear, because in that moment you know that life will never be the same as you knew it after the choice. And that there is something bigger than you that just screams: YES!

In 2007, I was a broker associate with a real estate firm in Pensacola, Florida, selling real estate during the market crash after Hurricane Katrina. Katrina trampled through the Panhandle and left little untouched, totally flipping our economy, our real estate, our lives, with total destruction. After Katrina, life as we knew it before had changed. The devastation turned the real estate market upside down. The homes that were still standing with minimal damage tripled in value, while blue tarps covered most roofs instead of shingles. Mortgage companies raised the qualifying bar and needless to say, unless I had a cash buyer, I wasn't closing any sales any time soon.

It did not take me long to realize that with no closings, as a single breadwinner of four, I had to make other financial choices quickly. I had already started utilizing Angel Food Ministries (they are such a blessing to so many), and I had already had been in contact with different institutions to help financially. It was apparent that resources, including my minimal savings, were drying up, which meant this independent little woman had to make some challenging choices. A friend of mine said: "Why don't you try pharmaceutical sales, you would be great at that!" My response was, "That is just cute in a suit and is not me!" However, my money was gone, resources were minimal, and I had three boys that needed food, clothing, and rent paid monthly, so I researched "cute in a suit" and came to find out that the pay was pretty good. So this "1099 little free bird" orchestrated her resume and began the process of applying for every pharmaceutical position available in the Panhandle, for three months. Yes, three months, and despite much successful sales experience, an outgoing personality, and a making life happen attitude, I got no call-backs, no interest. And I was frustrated beyond words.

So, one rainy day after three months of job seeking, after I had I taken the boys to school, I climbed back into bed to hide for the day, just for one day, from the fierce world that we call life. After all, I wasn't worth the call back, and I had bills to pay. The responsibilities were overwhelming and I just wanted to pull the covers over my head and hide. But no, my friend Samantha called me and said, "Get your ass up out of bed, I am coming over; this is not who you are!"

I thank God for friends that are real enough to offend me and to speak the truth when I needed it the most, because I was withering, beaten down, feeling unworthy, and she called me out, and uplifted me. Within an hour Samantha was at my house and we revised my resume. Then I began applying for additional pharmaceutical positions daily and continuously for the next two months.

Finally, I received a call from a recruiter; she was interested in me and had the perfect position. She told me that there was a contract position available, and that I needed to be in Washington D.C. in two days, get ready. So the race was on! I had no idea what to expect, since this was really my first corporate interview. Nonetheless, I made arrangements for the boys and I prepared my resume packets for the interviewers. The day came. I arrived in D.C., dressed in my new black suit, prepared to interview for the day and fly home with my new career I was manifesting before I even knew who I was.

When I arrived at the hotel where the interview took place, I was escorted up to a holding room full of black suits, beautiful people, full potential, previous pharmaceutical potential at that, and I was overwhelmed with anxiety. I went to the restroom, reminded myself of who I am, (*This is my day*, I told myself). I wiped the sweat from my face and applied powder to relinquish the shine. I exhaled. I thought, *I got this*.

The interview process was intense: the first hour I interviewed with two corporate people and since I made it through that interview, I went on to the next hour-long interview, with a different suit and different questions. The day seemed to be the longest ever. I went into the next room, two black suits, stuffy; the air thick. My energy surprised them but the interviewers chuckled at me because of my lack of experience; they did recognize who I was until I opened my mouth. I went hour-by-hour, interview-by-interview, pharmaceutical potential weaned out, while I continued.

Finally, during the last hour, one man in a Giorgio Armani suit in a room with me. I sat across from him, crossed my legs and exhaled. As my eyes locked with his, I knew I wasn't leaving this room without my job. It eventually came down to two candidates and from the beginning I knew this was not a bad run for a rookie, but the job wasn't mine yet. I left the room with a knowing; I knew I had the job beyond all knowing.

When the phone rang I answered with excitement and anticipation, after all I had been screening calls since I flew back from D.C., awaiting my confirmation. "Jenifer, I am so pleased to offer you a position with a contract pharmaceutical company for the Orlando, Florida territory." It was one of those moments in life when YES flies off the end of your tongue and then you realize you have three weeks to petition the court (for custody), find a house, register three boys in new schools, transfer all medical information, basically find a new life, while trying to prepare for a new career. I immediately called my attorney, letting him know that we needed an emergency hearing. I had interviewed for Pensacola, but they gave me Orlando for some reason, and I was told I had three weeks until I started.

So there I was standing on the edge of life, screaming while exhaling and feeling more alive than ever. This is why I wrote: *And the day came when she stood at the edge of life, trusted her cape of faith, and jumped.* After all, that is what happened without me even knowing—I jumped. I trusted. Something bigger was calling me and I knew I had to just do it. How would things be different now if, in a state of fear, I had said *no* because of the unknown, and remained stuck? I had no option but to move beyond my comfort zone, challenge the fear of the unknown, and defy everything that I had always known as true, which left me wanting.

This experience made me see that when you trust and you jump, amazing things happen. Divine intervention takes over and makes it all happen effortlessly. I was able to get everything in alignment for my move in three weeks. I drove down to Orlando in a U-Haul with my family on a Friday (looking a lot like the "Beverly Hillbillies," I suspect) and began my new job on Monday. Looking back it blows my mind how divine intervention without fear produces amazing results. Just yielding and trusting that still small voice (or sometimes loud overbearing voice) that says *yes* without your permission, opens the door of opportunity for life without fear to manifest.

Meditative Journaling—Chapter 5

1. *Why am I afraid to love or be loved?*
2. *How can I overcome my fear of dying?*
3. *How can I overcome living life small and conquer my fear of life?*

Chapter 6

Living Life Consciously

No problem can be solved from the same level of consciousness that created it.

~Albert Einstein

Nothing in our lives can be changed from the same level of awareness or awake-ness that created it. To create the changes in our lives that are desired, we need to be able to recognize our past. For years, we have been asleep— living and not paying attention to the big picture, and then waking up feeling stuck and unable to breathe. We have forgotten who we are, which has created an illusion of separation.

Living life consciously is about removing the idea of separateness from God and living fully in the moment, which is all we have. The definition of "conscious" is *aware of one's own existence, sensations, thoughts, or surroundings.* Another definition is *awake and able to understand what is happening around you, that which is known or felt by yourself.* I love the second definition of *conscious* because we truly do have to awaken to better understand what is happening around us and why. We should ask ourselves: *From what place are we creating?*

There are four basic concepts that I would like to focus on to help each and every person become more aware of the NOW and to live life consciously every day—and these will be expounded on in this chapter.

1) Stop blaming yourself for yesterday

2) Stop worrying about tomorrow (you miss today)

3) Slow down to feel life flowing through you, while seeing the joy in every day

4) Stop functioning in autopilot mode and you will be more aware.

> *What your attention is upon, you become.*
> ~*I Am Discourses,* Guy Ballard

When we are blaming ourselves for yesterday, or worrying about tomorrow, we miss today, the here and now, which is all we have. Living life consciously means we begin to understand why we have walked through what we have walked through in the past. When awareness begins to shine and we start understanding the lessons, or bigger picture, we begin to understand events and circumstances that have taken place in our lives for a higher purpose. In that awareness or awake-ness, we also begin to stop worrying about tomorrow because our knowing identifies we are all that we need inside— whole, nothing missing, nothing broken, set apart for such a time as this. When we live in this awareness (awake-ness) it's as if we are just flowing in the river of life, but when we are stuck in the past or worrying about the future, it's as if we are swimming upstream constantly, which is exhausting.

Living life consciously means adopting the awareness of all things, including the bad, ugly or indifferent, and releasing. Just let go and BE HERE NOW. It's the resistance that causes stress in our lives. When we arise to the awareness of truth in all things we can truly be present, which is the best present we can offer ourselves or another.

The Merriam-Webster Dictionary defines "awake-ness" as *the quality or state of being wide-awake.* To live life consciously is to live it in awake-ness, which is BE-ing wide awake to who you are and aware of that place which you create from. Living in the past is only creating more of what you have experienced in the past. I witnessed this in the safe house and even in my own life. Some of the women would come in for one day, maybe two, but could not identify or imagine their lives any other way than filled with abuse or mistreatment, and consequently went back to recreate the same life they had been living from the illusion of fear.

In my own life, I blamed myself and looked outside of myself for the Love I desired, which was in me all along. Even in the silent blame from yesterday, we are haunted and re-creating the past (in the now) and we are in a state of sleep. I recognize that place all too well. It haunted me for years: *not being enough, my boys not having their dad in the home, how I should have stayed with my husband no matter what,* and all the other ways a perfectionist can beat herself up. Oh, and then there is the worry about tomorrow and the *what if. What if I don't have enough money to pay my bills? What if my boys always blame me?*

I could go on, but I believe you get the point. I was in a state of sleep, unaware that my self-inflicted torment was recreating more misery for myself because I wasn't creating from Love or from my source. I was creating from my illusion of fear or lack. I was creating from that negative chatter that never seemed to be quiet within the walls of my mind. After all, I had always lived like this and everyone I know lives like this, so that is the way we are supposed to live, right? Absolutely not! It is the shift that makes the difference, the moment your awareness is awakened to the truth of who you are, which is LOVE.

All that I have ever believed myself to be, all that I now believe myself to be, and all that I shall ever believe myself to be, are but great attempts to know myself—the unknown undefined Reality.

~Neville Goddard

I love this quote by Neville Goddard, on which I would like to elaborate. Personally, all that I have ever believed myself to be was based on how others perceived me, what I was conditioned to believe, or what I filtered from my environment to identify with. All that I now believe myself to be is my current awareness, and the shift from yesterday's belief to today's belief, still based on my knowing. All that I shall ever believe myself to be is the future self projected, in full awake-ness. Similarly, this is all of mankind's unknown quest to understand reality, which is to understand ourselves.

Living life consciously is to slow down, to recognize the spaces between the breaths. How many of our days have gone unnoticed?

Like "Groundhog Day," each day is the same over and over. We get up and go, not even paying attention, just running through the motions to pay the bills. For what? To get up tomorrow and do it again until our last breath of regret. Living life consciously is the intention behind the list of things to do. The "so what" behind the motions.

For me, it was the recognition that I was not a number, nor was I doing anything to exceed a quota that played a part in my waking up. I am in sales, and quotas are what we are supposed to increase every quarter, but I had to shift my awareness so that I could see that my intentions never change, regardless of the quota. My intentions are to serve. In my awake-ness to my intentions, I could actually slow down to feel life flowing through me. I could see and recognize joy in everyday moments, the breeze on my skin, the warmth of the sun, a child's laughter. These simple things we miss if we are unconscious, just pushing through time, day after day, until it is gone. "Unconscious" is defined as *the part of the mind that is inaccessible to the conscious mind but affects behaviors and emotions.* Even our un-knowing or unconsciousness affects how we feel or how we respond to life. So isn't it better to live life on purpose? To arise and recognize that there is so much more to this life than just going through the motions. In this slowing down, we allow life to be present with joy, which is there all the time but we are so busy that we miss it.

This idea of stopping to take notice is exemplified in a video I recently saw posted on Facebook, of a boy sitting on a bench out in the freezing cold. As each stranger came up to sit beside him, the boy shivering with nothing on his arms, each person had their own way of helping him—by either giving him a jacket or scarf, or a hat. But this boy and these acts of kindness toward him would have gone unnoticed if we were racing along. If that person didn't capture that moment in a video, then post it, to remind us to slow down and pay attention, we would not remember. The point is that life is happening all around us, we just have to slow down so we do not miss it.

When I was going to college, I had a professor ask the class a question that I will never forget. One day he asked the entire class to take out a piece of paper and write down the details of exactly how we had arrived to class that day. All the expressions around the room were similar; we were all thinking maybe the professor just wasn't prepared for the lecture. Regardless, we all wrote down how we arrived to class that morning. After about fifteen minutes, he went around the room and asked several of the students to share what they had written. Of course, no one really understood what the point was, but we still shared anyway. After several people had read, the instructor revealed why he had us write down the details of how we had gotten to class that day. To begin with, he told us that there are many different ways to arrive at the same destination; no right or wrong way to arrive, just different pathways depending on location or perception.

Then, he asked us to count how many traffic lights we went through daily to arrive at school and if there was anything that happened in our life on a weekly basis that we could remember. Thinking about this, most of us quickly realized that it was difficult to respond to how many lights we went through to get to class, three times a week, some of us for years. Most of us didn't even notice! It seemed that the reality was that we were already on autopilot, in college, and hadn't even begun to live our lives yet.

I was completely in awe, in disbelief, that I was so thoroughly unaware, already in a hypnotized state. After all, I was the hippie girl who took her shoes off in between classes and walked on the grass. Regardless, I was on autopilot, as was most of the class. Just simply going through the motions of life and missing it.

Autopilots are used in aircraft, boats, spacecraft, missiles, and with many other machines, but I want to focus on airplanes. Autopilots do not replace a human operator, but assist them in controlling the vehicle, allowing them to focus on broader aspects of operation, such as weather. So, just what is it that we are focusing on when we live our lives on autopilot? We are not focused on the broader aspect of our lives or higher levels of thinking. We are numb and zoned out to the beauty of even being alive.

Recently, I was in New York for Thanksgiving with my love and to just sit on a bench for fifteen minutes in New York can provide a clear example of people going through the day on autopilot. Everyone was in a hurry, racing along, never looking up to smile, talking fast on cell phones, bumping into each other, and sad. *Where has the happiness gone? Why is there is so much depression and loneliness?* Love, it is time to take life off of the autopilot mode and throw it into Neutral. Slow down and pay attention to the intentions behind what you do and why. When we place life in Neutral we give ourselves permission to "feel" again and to find the beauty. This is living life consciously, on purpose, and feeling your way through, as opposed to racing through. Living life with love and with all the senses. The end will be here before we know it. Have you ever met someone on their deathbed that regretted living too much? Most regret not living, working too much, and realizing how much they missed when it is too late. Conscious living is calling you to throw it into Neutral and enjoy the moments you have been gifted with.

For me it took relocating to Orlando and beginning my new life in pharmaceutical sales to notice that I wasn't living life consciously. It is so easy to get caught up in Corporate America—chasing a quota and trying to be more. I would wake up day after day, doing the same thing, and on a fast track that just kept repeating, while not writing one word toward my dream. Even though my boys were doing amazing, I had a great home, an awesome job with wonderful benefits, I didn't realize how quickly I had become hypnotized. I fell asleep to life. I stepped into Corporate America, "living the dream," and stressed myself beyond reason to prove to myself and the world that I was enough. Until one day when I received the news that the entire contract sales force was being laid off. Friday would be my last day of employment. I remember the fear that consumed my mind. *Oh my God, I have relocated my life, I have an expensive rental and now I have no job.* I remember thinking that I loaded our lives up in a U-Haul and moved down to Florida like the Beverly Hillbillies; *wasn't that enough God?*

Still, I stood on the edge of life, trusted you with all that I am, and jumped. If we get consumed with life, then life can sometimes awaken us if we pay attention. The Universe has a remarkable way of making us more conscious if we will just listen. It's moments like these in our lives when our soul is being shaken to awaken and pay attention, recognizing what needs to be seen and embraced with open arms.

After the layoff, I spent the next month applying for every pharmaceutical position available. My aunt kept telling me I was on a paid vacation and to just relax. However, this "Type A, make life happen" little lady could not embrace the notion that I was on a vacation. All I could think and worry about was that I had bills to pay and children to take care of and I needed to make something happen. I did not take time to be in the moment, breathe, and ask God why I was in this position.

I kept "stressing on" and applying for all available jobs. Three weeks into my so-called "vacation," I received a phone call from my previous pharmaceutical manager. I was standing in the FedEx office sending off another resume package for an upcoming interview when I answered the call. "Jen, this is Mike and I wanted to offer you a permanent full-time position with the company." I told him if I wasn't in the FedEx store I would have screamed at the top of my lungs. Of course, I accepted!

I asked myself then, *What if I would have known (had the awareness) that everything was going to work out for the best? Would I have been so stressed? Could I have exhaled and just relaxed into the flow and river of life?* I had to realize then, and I have to remind myself now, to live life consciously. It is too easy to be who we have always been, which for me was that "Type A, make life happen" little lady, instead of living in awareness that all is good and manifesting for the better of the whole—that is for you and for all. It's the knowing that there is a Divine Energy at work, flowing through all of life, like the flowing river of awareness, which we are meant to flow into, not against.

> *When you do things from your soul, you feel a river moving in you, a Joy...*
>
> ~Rumi

Meditative Journaling—Chapter 6

1. *How can I begin to live my life more consciously?*

2. *What in me needs attention to live life effortlessly?*

Chapter 7

Heaven or Hell: A Present Reality

Love in your mind produces love in your life. This is the meaning of heaven. Fear in your mind produces fear in your life. This is the meaning of hell.

~Marianne Williamson, *A Return to Love*

The way we respond to or react to life does not determine whether we go to heaven or hell when we die. The way we respond to or react to life creates our present reality: heaven or hell. It is what we endure on a daily basis. We get so caught up in our suffering that we fail to realize that our thoughts and reactions to life created our current circumstances. This is literally the spiritual visualization of cause and effect.

The spiritual law of cause and effect is simply this: What we send out comes back. Every action, thought, or feeling produces an effect in life. You've probably heard the statement, "You are what you eat." Actually, you are what you think and feel—this is your reality. Understanding the power behind the statement— you are what you think and feel—is so important, but completely missed unless you own it. Even if you are unconscious you are still creating your life. "Conscious mind" is defined as *aware of or awake*. A conscious mind is a mind that *chooses* to be aware and is awakened to how that knowing impacts reality. Further we might inquire, is it a conscious mind or a conscious awareness beyond the mind that creates our experiences on the earth?

This concept is completely different from what I was conditioned to believe my entire life. As a child, I can remember praying to God to forgive me because I was a sinner, and consequently begging for Him to let me go to heaven. I did this weekly at church. Each week, I would beg prayerfully for forgiveness and ask to go to heaven. The fear behind the prayer and my lack of knowing makes my heart sad, but it was all necessary to bring me to this present point of awake-ness.

One of my spiritual mentors shared this truth with me: heaven or hell is a present reality. From that moment, it seemed as if every spiritual book I read conveyed the same message. From texts by Marianne Williamson to Neville Goddard to Lillian De Waters— each emphasized the same understanding. *When the student is ready the teacher appears* and when my teacher appeared to present this truth, I was ready to receive it. It is as if everything in my life had prepared me for every moment to know the truth and go beyond the limitations of conditioning. The beautiful realization is when you witness all that you have walked through, and all that you have learned, you can see this unspoken truth clearly. Life has been preparing for this recognizing moment all along.

As Rumi said, *"Those who don't want to change, let them sleep."* There is absolutely nothing wrong with where you are at on your current path or where you are going, as long as you own that you have chosen it. There is no judgment, only love. Everyone is exactly where they are supposed to be, doing exactly what they are supposed to be doing, and everyone has an *ah-ha* moment when ready.

> *Ideas are impressed on the subconscious through the medium of feeling. No idea can be impressed on the subconscious mind until felt, but once felt—be it good or bad or indifferent—it must be expressed. Feeling is the one and only medium through which ideas are conveyed to the subconscious."*
>
> ~Neville Goddard

So not only are you everything you think you are. You are everything you feel you are. Thoughts create feelings and feelings create thought. Love, we must learn to master our minds before we can master the world we create. We must master our thoughts and feelings if we want to create a heaven instead of a hell. How do we do that? It is simpler than we think, but it takes conscious minute-to-minute effort, and surrender to that which is higher within you, to start creating in an awareness of LOVE. Remember Marianne Williamson's quote: *"Love in your mind produces love in your life. This is the meaning of heaven. Fear in your mind produces fear in your life. This is the meaning of hell."*

The moment we surrender to the knowing of who we are, LOVE, and begin to look at the world as a reflection of that knowing, then heaven begins to manifest. Life will continue to happen and we will be challenged because we are learning the necessary lessons. *What would happen if we responded with love instead of fear? How would our lives be different? Would our lives change from a hell to a heaven?* We would still have bills, challenging family members, situations that push us to grow, but it is the way we react to life that would be different. When we respond in love, we vibrate higher, and our response affects everything around us.

During meditation, I asked God for guidance in writing this chapter. The next day, I had an image of the eye of the hurricane. Living in Florida all of my life I am very familiar with hurricanes, and I have experienced some pretty powerful ones during my lifetime. Regardless of how strong the winds are blowing, 120 or 160 miles an hour, Category 2 or a Category 4, destruction and debris everywhere, once the eye of the hurricane is over your location, it is calm, sunny, and beautiful. The only proof that the storm existed was the debris. Some descriptions of the eye of the hurricane are with skies that are often clear above the eye and winds that are relatively light. The eye is the calmest section of any hurricane; and the eye is so calm because the strong surface winds that converge toward the center never reach it.

This is the metaphor for us to follow in our lives. If we react or respond in fear, then we are whirling around in strong winds struggling to survive. If we react or respond in Love, then we are in the eye of the storm, and the strong winds never touch us, even though we understand they are there, because we choose to stay in the calm. It is always a choice. The symbolism behind the eye of the hurricane is so powerful when we think about it, similar to the idea that "we are in this world but not of it."

How many people do you know are currently living their daily lives as if they are in a ferocious hurricane? I would say most of the people I know, and yes the words just poured out onto the page: *be the eye in the midst of the storm.* Does that mean even on Thanksgiving Day, when dinner is at my house, family and friends and disagreements and all, I am to stay in the eye (I) and respond in Love? Or what about when someone slams into the back of my car because they are not paying attention? Yes, Yes, and Yes. Had I applied this concept to my life in all that I have experienced, how differently things would have been... How differently things would have been if I would have reacted in Love instead of Fear. There have been many moments in my life when I was completely consumed with fear and anguish and there was not one ounce of love flowing from me in that moment.

So how does one shift in real life? How could I have been in the eye of the hurricane when I had packed up all of my belongings into garbage bags and I had no idea where I was going or what tomorrow would bring? Being in the eye of the hurricane doesn't mean that the winds of life are not going to whirl around you, it just means that your experience with the situation will be different because you will be responding with love instead of fear. Our response may or may not influence other people around us or our environment immediately, but it does impact all things, especially you. If I had responded in love, then I would not have fallen on my face in despair during difficult times in my life, stressed my body out, went into victim mode and lost hours of sleep agonizing over how to resolve this situation immediately, while still trying to put my hands on life and solve all my problems. My experience of this earthly realm is my heaven or hell, just the same as yours.

When we respond with love, we begin to see with the eyes of love, and even if a person is trying to hurt or destroy you, the love in you is more powerful than the fear in the perpetrator. That is how we create our heaven. When I lost my job during the layoff,

I was whirling around in the hurricane. I was stressed beyond words, full of fear, and spinning out, trying to find the first position that could pay my bills and resolve this issue. My aunt kept telling me, "You're on vacation for a month." But, nothing in my mind could accept that statement. There was too much financial pressure on me to provide for my three boys and I was determined to find another job. So my experience of my life in that moment, consumed with fear and responding in fear, created my hell, which I didn't even realize I was living in.

How different would this situation have been if I would have responded in love? My reaction would have been less stressful on my physical body and I would have had a knowing that everything happens for a reason and all is well. Responding in love would have influenced my experience with being unemployed and maybe I could have trusted the process a little more; being in the eye of the hurricane instead of the winds.

For Heaven and Hell are within you, and reward and punishment are simply cause and effect in your use of the great spiritual laws that govern all life.

~Uell S. Anderson, *Three Magic Words*

This quote by Anderson brings us right back to the idea that our thoughts and feelings create our heaven or hell and it all starts within us. The result of thinking or feeling may be perceived as reward or punishment, but are simply the cause and effect of our own thinking.

The most valuable way we can influence our world is to master our thoughts and feelings. This is done by recognizing God within, becoming conscious of our thoughts and feelings continuously, and choosing to change thoughts and feelings that are negative and do not serve us well. This sounds extremely simple and yet the most profound lesson of all is to unlearn all that we have been conditioned to believe that has created separation from ourselves and the Divine within.

So start where you are at and awake to thoughts and feelings. Pay attention and shift as needed. We are all learning and processing and unlearning and going higher together, you are not alone.

You rise to a higher level of consciousness by taking your attention away from your present limitations and placing it upon that which you desire to be. Do not attempt this in day-dreaming or wishful thinking but in a positive manner. Claim yourself to be the thing desired. I am that; no sacrifice, no diet, no human tricks. All that is asked of you is to accept your desire. If you dare claim it, you will express it.

~Neville Goddard

This is the shift. Most of us spend the majority of our time thinking about the limitations and the negative, which creates more negative. The shift is taking your thoughts away from the limitations and focusing on what is desired, creating from a place of love, which manifests your heaven. It is our Divine Inheritance to live in beauty, abundance, joy, and peace, not a sacred privilege for the special. This is the Divine Inheritance, sacred privilege, for ALL, which is ONE mind, ONE soul, One consciousness on a journey of ONE to reach our heaven on earth, which is our Kingdom.

> *For you grow to heaven, you don't go to heaven. It is within thine own conscience that ye grow there."*
>
> ~Edgar Cayce

My love, as we grow through our life lessons, understanding each lesson on a higher level, we grow to heaven or we create a heaven on earth, which is our kingdom.

MEDITATIVE JOURNALING—CHAPTER 7

1. **Am I living in a hell or heaven and how have my thoughts and feelings manifested that?**
2. **How can I change my thoughts to create my heaven?**

Chapter 8

"I AM Manifested"

I AM (YOUR CONSCIOUSNESS)

~Neville Goddard

What a beautiful definition of I AM. I mentioned previously that the definition of "conscious" is *the understanding or awareness that enables us to realize what is happening around us.* So the I AM, my consciousness, is the awareness and knowing of that which flows through me. In that understanding, we know what is happening around us and why. To Learn. To Shift. To Go and grow Higher. As we progress and expand our awareness, this knowing shifts the people that we are around, as well as our environment. Thinking about Neville Goddard's statement "I AM is your consciousness" reinforces the relevance of the power behind the words I AM. It is that silent place within our soul that we create from. The great Persian poet, Jalāl ad-Dīn Muhammad Rumi said, *"When you do things from your soul, you feel a river moving in you, a Joy."* I believe living the I AM is when you create from your soul, and in that creating, the river of joy flows through you to bless the world. If we don't recognize who the I

AM is within each and every one of us, then we are creating our world from a sense of separation or a lack of knowing. Separation is lack of connection with all and God. That lack of knowing or awareness is the reason why we do not claim heaven, the reason that suffering is experienced.

> *What we do not claim, remains invisible.*
>
> ~Marianne Williamson, *A Return to Love*

I absolutely love this quote by Marianne Williamson. The depth behind the words can be felt on so many levels. And I connected *"what we do not claim, remains invisible"* with every lesson discussed in this book (from LOVING THE GODDESS WITHIN to I AM MANIFESTED). *How can we love the Goddess within if we do not claim our Divinity? How do we love what is invisible?* If we don't claim that we are Goddesses, Divine, Love Manifested, and Worthy with a knowing beyond all knowing, then it remains invisible or nonexistent. We have to claim it, own it, to make the invisible visible. *How do we live the I AM if we do not claim who we are as a spiritual being? If we are unaware of the very one who exists behind the clothes, job title, ethnicity, or family background, then how can we live from the place of higher consciousness?*

I spent several weeks in deep thought and meditation on living the I AM. *What does it look like? How does one successfully live it? How do we even know if I am living my I AM or your I AM?* Thoughts and ideas continued to dance in my brain. After all, I write myself into my own healing and understanding, going higher in consciousness with every word that flows from that silent place within. One night I meditated, asking God to show me and give me the understanding so I can BE what it is that I write. As soon as my eyes opened, God had given me the answer. The most Divine example, so simple, yet complex. I was so completely overwhelmed with emotion and a power behind the knowing that embraced my soul that I cried. *Thank you,* I whispered. God gave me my I AM, which translates into other I AM's in this beautiful environment of souls we live among.

I AM THE WORDS THAT FLOW THROUGH ME; I WRITE TO REMEMBER.

These are the majestic words God gave me. I was already my I AM MANIFESTED — every time I picked up my pen to write, just BE-ing. I didn't even realize that I was already living the very thing I was seeking, even writing to remind myself. If I didn't have this awareness or knowing, then how could I claim it or live it? The simplicity behind the words is so amazing, yet powerfully overwhelming. The awareness that flowed from this knowing painted the most beautiful picture of the souls that we are. I AM the love that flows through me, I love to remember. I AM the song that bellows from within. I sing to remember. I AM the healer inside. I heal to remember.

After God gave me these beautiful words I began to feel beyond the definition Neville Goddard described as "I AM=YOUR CONSCIOUSNESS." I began exploring the idea that when we are utilizing gifts of the spirit: love, peace, joy, humbleness, and service, we are in the one body, one mind, universal consciousness, which could be the Universal I AM. I AM MANIFESTED is God flowing through you, with your individual talent, that you may or may not be acknowledging yet, but your I AM is waiting to be claimed and manifested.

When we flow from our source, that place of joy and love, we are living our I AM. I AM MANIFESTED is God in motion, flowing through each person reflecting perfection, beauty, and bliss at its highest, to awaken all into Divinity. This is our Kingdom, within. And it is the acknowledgment that brings it forth. Living the I AM is beautiful and for each and every one of us, but also serving the whole in the most glorious way. When I write truly, my pen just flows, the words pour out from this higher source onto the page. Most of the time when I re-read what I have written, I am in awe and gratitude. When I write, my joy flows. I am balanced, and I feel this innate knowing that I am doing something right and something that will make a positive difference. When I slow down to BE in my awareness, which means I turn off my A.D.D. and just breathe, I know, which is when I truly write. When I force myself to sit and agonize over facing a blank page, then I am not living my I AM. That is the difference. The doing versus the un-doing. The natural flow versus putting your hands on it and making it happen. This is what I have been doing my entire life, putting my hands on it and making it happen.

I had a mentor fifteen years ago that I worked with while I was selling real estate as a broker associate. He was an investor and bought homes at a great price, gutted each one, and then either sold or rented them. Since I was fairly new to the real estate business, he took me under his wing, taught me how to improve market value to make the most profit, taught me how to measure a room, about the structure that was beneath the walls, and how to tear down walls to build new ones.

I will never forget one Saturday morning; we met at seven a.m. to begin tearing down drywall in this house he had just purchased. We always talked while we worked; it felt like impromptu therapy sessions, reflecting on life and sharing perspectives—with his wisdom always rising. On this day, he looked at me and made a statement that I have literally pondered and held onto for fifteen years. He said, "Jen, you have to get out of your own way!" He didn't explain exactly what he meant and I literally put down my sledge hammer to take in the moment. (We were both physically tearing down walls as he spoke to me.) After he made the statement, I continued to tear down a wall with my sledge hammer, while thinking of all the means by which I could possibly be in my own way.

Little insight came to me then. But for years his words were dormant in my mind, awaiting the right moment of awareness for manifestation. I just remembered his statement right now, while writing this chapter. For my entire life, I have been serving that small self, the little girl inside of me, not acknowledging who I am or the God in me. My awareness now has made me realize that serving the small self and not the God self is why I had fear—this was myself getting in my own way. Always focusing on what I could or could not do, forgetting to acknowledge the who behind the I. The ego silently ruling all along, until I decided to own and claim that part of myself which knows I can do "no-thing," but through God I can do all things.

I Can Do All Things Through Christ Who Strengthens Me.

~Philippians 4:13

BE-ing the I AM has been my most challenging life lesson of all. I have to completely unlearn everything I have been conditioned to believe, to truly live my I AM. I was always taught that I was a sinner and unworthy of God's love and forgiveness, to pray to a God out there, and that if I repented and asked God into my heart then I would go to heaven.

There is absolutely nothing wrong with religious doctrine if that is what you choose to learn from. Religious doctrine was in fact the vessel for leading me to this moment as I write these words and live my I AM, for which I am grateful. However, unlearning daily is my biggest challenge. I must constantly remind myself that I am the hands and feet of God and there is no separation. It is a knowing that I choose to live in my heaven, which is my Divine birthright and that I can choose to live in hell if I change my mind. If I choose to get on the ride of negativity, gossip, thoughts of lack, or self-judgment, then that is my hell, which is a separation from I AM and the powerful Love that resides within. So living in heaven is a daily choice, as well as the realization that of myself I can do nothing, but yielding to the powerful God force inside me, then I can do all things, which includes mastering my mind to live in my heaven.

Since I was a child, I was taught that I was a sinner, and unworthy of God's love and forgiveness. This thought breaks my heart for that place where I have been and for all those who are still there. How can I be unworthy of something that I AM?

I recently went to church and I was surprised to hear those words in a prayer, "Lord I am not worthy." My *ah-ha* moment of realization happened right there in that church.

I had been silently believing that lie and beating myself up with it for years, now I know why. I am worthy, as are you!! I am Love, as are you!! If Jesus died on the cross 2,000 years ago for my sins, then why am I a sinner and need to beg for forgiveness? IT IS FINISHED! I am free and so are you in that knowing. It is the dogma or unquestioned belief which keeps us in the dark and suffering. Turn the light on and rise up!! Lillian De Waters wrote, "Inevitably, so long as one is engaged in looking, his search is perpetual and endless. Yet the looking is not altogether fruitless if he comes finally to the place where he completely surrenders all effort, struggle and search. At this point of his extremity comes his great opportunity. Like a man waking from deep slumber, his eyes open and see, his ears are attuned and hear, his integrity is restored, and he knows the Truth—I am that for which I have searched.....I Am That I Am."

This is so profound and so accurately describes my journey up to this point. Nothing that I have "grown" through, studied, read, and struggled for has been in vain because it brought me to this moment of understanding that I AM all that I have searched for and longed for. Instead of looking outside of myself for explanations or for answers, I am looking inside, which is all Truth and is my source. The I AM in me is the I AM in you—we just have to look inward to witness and claim it.

Living the I AM is letting go and letting God. It is total surrender to that beautiful life force that is within you, God. It is the awareness, accepting that knowing and claiming it, which is your

Divine inheritance; to know who you are and live it. When I claim it and live it, then I give you permission and transfer authority for you to live it. When you claim it and live it, then you give the next person permission and the transfer of authority to live it.

What does I AM MANIFESTED look like in real life? I can almost hear your thoughts because it is the negative chatter I battle every day to overcome. I remember driving my son to school several days ago during a bad storm with extremely strong winds. The lake was ferocious and huge ocean-like waves were crashing upon the bank. The storm lasted for several days, blowing down branches and moss. After the storm passed, neighbors were out cleaning up and preparing for the next storm. Today, while driving my son to school, the lake was calm and glassy, a complete beautiful reflection of life. This is a perfect example of the before and after my I AM MANIFESTED experience. My "before" experience was that the winds of life were strong, beating me up and knocking me down, and it was exhausting. I didn't realize that I was creating my life from a place of low vibration with lack of love. I was an example of "a man waking from deep slumber." I was like my neighbors, constantly cleaning up the mess I had created without awareness, and I was always bracing myself for the next storm of life. After all, that is what we do, as single moms, raising children on our own—we bow down and take life on to make it happen.

Until one day utterly exhausted and done, we surrender to something more, something bigger than ourselves that we don't quite understand yet, because it is everything that we have *not* been taught, but it is still all too familiar to deny. I had to release the delusion that I was not able and enough to be everything I thought I needed to be. The key word is "thought." My "after" is a peaceful surrender to that beautiful powerful source, which is GOD within that carries the burden, lights the path, and keeps me in the NOW. My "after" is the words that flow through me to give and bless, all while writing myself into my own healing daily. My "after" is life flowing like a river and I am flowing in it, in my joy, instead of swimming upstream. This is my desire and prayer for you, that you will surrender and claim your I AM. Exhale and let go.

My prayer is full of gratitude and praise for the words that flow through me from the Divine. I yield this vessel for your glory, for your love, and for your highest purpose. May I BE the words that flow through me and may I be of service to heal. Shalom. So to help identify your I AM, ask yourself, God, in your journal *"What is it that is beautiful and amazing about me that flows when I am not paying attention?"* The most important part of the statement here is, "when I am not paying attention." When we are not thinking is when we are most aligned with spirit—it's the mind, or "stinking thinking" that creates separation from God or emphasizes our EGO.

For myself, I had too many things going on in my world and in my head to hear. Going back to the image of the lake, I was struggling, barely coming up for air, waves crashing, and branches falling all around me. I just kept running, doing anything and everything just to numb the pain. There is no silence in our lives if our lake is roaring with violent waves. From television to radio to kids to jobs and phone calls, the list goes on and on—with absolutely no room for silence. So how can we hear or know that which is within us if we are so consumed with noise, static, and confusion?

I had to turn off the television, in my head and in my life. Literally, I discontinued watching daily television first. And just recently, I stopped listening to the radio. No, I am not trying to become a monk or live in isolation; but for me, once I experienced the silence, the "after," I just desired and desire more. The silence makes it easier for me to stay connected with my source, which is your source and it is what works for me. This may not be your solution, because we are all are on our own unique journey. My desire is that you will discover your own way to connect within and overcome the battering winds in your own life, ultimately healing and giving others permission to do the same.

Our challenge is to bring that wholeness to consciousness, an "awareness within each soul, imprinted in pattern on the mind and waiting to be awakened by the will, of the soul's oneness with God."

~Edgar Cayce

This is one of our most challenging lessons of all, to bring our awareness to consciousness to be made whole. As Cayce states, it is already within each soul, we just have to unlearn what we have "learned" to open ourselves up to choose. It is our choice always, and we have been gifted with free will. Once we choose, and recognize what has been imprinted upon our hearts all along, we will align and be with One with God, the essence of each soul. We all are spiritual beings having a human experience, learning life lessons to remember we are spiritual beings. The following "I AM" poem came to me years ago and was the beginning of this book. As these words flow from me, I was brought back to the poem to reflect on a deeper meaning; to finish this chapter and to help lift the veil that obscures your sight. God is so funny and life is a complete circle.

God I AM

The God in me is more than what I see...more than what I think....and more than I can imagine.

The God in me is full of Beauty and Grace awaiting exposure. The God in me is life in all its fullness. The God in me is all I need inside...strong...determined... and ready!

The God in me is Love. Love in its truest form because He dwells in the walls of my soul...penetrates the chambers of my heart...and projects through my every action, word, or thought.

The God in me is an amazing ...demonstrating the characteristics all contain, but fail to reveal or claim.

The God in me is enough...in everything that I do... everything I say...and in all that I dream...

I AM.

As these words flowed, I had to pause and catch my breath, tears arising from deep within, in complete awe of the beauty, the connection. I had no idea that the poem would be used to connect with the I AM. This is the truest example of my "after," my God I AM MANIFESTED. Jenifer taking her hands off of it and letting go, just letting God do it, and exhaling.

Love, these words are for you as they are for me. Just let Go and let God. As we are on this journey of One together, learning, healing, and going higher, remember you are not alone and you are so much more than you can imagine. I wish you Love, Light, and Blessings.

Meditative Journaling—Chapter 8

1. *What is preventing me from living my I AM?*
2. *How can I begin to witness the I AM in my life?*
3. *When have I witnessed the I AM in my life already?*

Recommended Readings

Anderson, Uell. *Three Magic Words*. Snowball Publishing. 2012.

Ballard, Guy. *The I AM Discourses*. Volumes 1-20. Schaumburg, IL: Saint Germain Press. 1930.

Ban Breathnach, Sara. *Something more: Excavating Your Authentic Self*. New York: Warner Books. 1995.

Goddard, Neville. The Power of Awareness. New York: Penguin Group. 1952.

Murphy, Joseph, MD. *The Power of Your Subconscious Mind*. UK: Penguin Random House. 2009.

Ruiz, Miguel. The Mastery of Love: A Practical Guide to the Art of Relationship. A Toltec Wisdom Book. San Rafael, CA. 1999.

Selig, Paul. *The Book of Love and Creation*. New York: Penguin Group. 2012.

Selig, Paul. T*he Book of Mastery*. New York: Penguin Random House. 2016.

Weiss, Brian, PhD. Many Lives, Many Masters. New York: Simon & Schuster. 1990.

Williamson, Marianne. A Return to Love. New York, NY: Harper Collins. 1999.

New books from River Sanctuary Publishing...

God Is: Ending Hell with a Course in Miracles, by George Provost. 2017. $18.95

And the Earth Spoke: True stories to inspire and awaken, channeled messages from nature by Ashalyn, 2016. $23.95

Living as Prayer; Meditations for any day...any time...any thing, by Unity prayer chaplain Bobbie Spivey. 2016 $9.95

Scent of Love, a poetic celebration of the feminine, by Dominique Rose. 2016 $12.95

Other Favorites

Love, Alba (a novel), by former NY Times bestselling author Sophy Burnham, 2015. $15.95

A Goddess Journal, (blank journal with illustrations and affirmations) by Melanie Gendron and Annie Elizabeth, 2015. $12.95

River Sanctuary Publishing
P.O. Box 1561
Felton, California 95018
www.riversanctuarypublishing.com
(831) 335-7283

We offer custom book design and production with worldwide availability through print-on-demand, with personalized service and the most author-favorable terms in the industry. Specializing in inspirational, spiritual and self-help books, biography, and memoirs.

www.ingramcontent.com/pod-product-compliance
Lightning Source LLC
LaVergne TN
LVHW011426080426
835512LV00005B/286